CRITICAL GUIDES TO SPANISH TEXTS

I

Pérez Galdós: Doña Perfecta

CRITICAL GUIDES TO SPANISH TEXTS

Edited by

J. E. Varey and A. D. Deyermond

PÉREZ GALDÓS

DOÑA PERFECTA

*

J. E. VAREY

*Professor of Spanish in the University of London
at Westfield College*

Grant & Cutler Ltd
in association with
Tamesis Books Ltd
1971

© Grant & Cutler Ltd
1971

SBN 900411 22 8

Depósito legal: M.-12882-1971

Printed in Spain by Talleres Gráficos de Ediciones Castilla, S.A.
Maestro Alonso, 23 - Madrid

for

GRANT & CUTLER LTD
11 BUCKINGHAM STREET, LONDON W.C.2.

Contents

References

All references to the text of *Doña Perfecta* are to Vol. IV of the *Obras completas* of Benito Pérez Galdós, ed. F. C. Sainz de Robles, 7th ed. (Madrid, 1969). Each reference gives the chapter number followed by the page.

The figures in brackets in bold type refer to the numbered items in the Bibliographical Note; the bold figure is followed by a page reference.

I

Introduction

As a man, Galdós was shy and retiring; as a writer, he found himself in the centre of political, social and religious controversies. He first achieved prominence through the *Episodios nacionales,* the first series of which was published between 1873 and 1875. When, with *Doña Perfecta* (1876), *Gloria* (1876-1877) and *La familia de León Roch* (1878), he turned to novels set in contemporary Spain, he awoke the enthusiasm of liberal reformers and provoked attacks by those conservatives who dreaded the submersion of what they considered to be the old Spanish virtues under a wave of foreign ideas and influences. In 1897, in his speech welcoming Galdós on his election to the Spanish Academy, the Conservative critic Menéndez y Pelayo spoke with warmth of the first series of the *Episodios nacionales,* and then turned to the historical and political novels of what Galdós himself termed his "primera época". Of *Gloria* and *La familia de León Roch* Menéndez y Pelayo observed:

> Esas novelas no fueron juzgadas en cuanto a su valor artístico: fueron exaltadas o maldecidas con igual furor y encarnizamiento, por los que andaban metidos en la batalla de ideas de que aquellos libros eran trasunto.[1]

The critical reception of these three novels is recorded by Berkowitz in his biography of the novelist (1, 135-149). For the first time since the seventeenth century, Spain had produced a novelist capable of confronting his readers with living issues in a manner and style which were authentically modern. One of Galdós's greatest achievements was, in fact, the creation of a reading public no longer content with the serialised late-Romantic historical novels of writers such as

---

[1]*Discursos leídos ante la Real Academia Española en las recepciones públicas del 7 y 21 de febrero de 1897*(Madrid, 1897), 71-72.

Fernández y González.

The very success of these works, and the polemics aroused in the 1890s by Galdós's plays —one of which was his own dramatisation of *Doña Perfecta,* first performed in 1896— tended to obscure the value of the "novelas de la primera época" in the eyes of contemporary and later critics. In the 1920s, the *Historia de la literatura española* of Hurtado and Palencia, for example, lumps together Galdós's novels and treats them as though all deal with the same themes as *Doña Perfecta:*

> Su mérito principal es el poder extraordinario de observación: brilla más en la pintura de caracteres y descripciones de tipos y lugares (sobre todo de la clase media y baja) que en la acción y movimiento de las pasiones. Sus tipos característicos son: uno, simpático, que representa el progreso, la luz, el agrado (el ingeniero joven); otro, antipático, símbolo del obscurantismo, tal como lo entiende Galdós (el sacerdote): ambos están admirablemente contrapuestos en *Doña Perfecta.* Idealista a veces en su representación del mundo, es frío, y no tiene llama lírica (2nd ed. [Madrid 1925], 1020).

The same attitude persisted throughout the 1920s, when Galdós was ridiculed by such writers as Valle-Inclán, who called him "Don Benito, el garbancero",[2] and his works were attacked as stodgy and unreadable. A new revaluation of his output had to await the centenary of his birth, and it was in 1943 that critics began seriously to reread his works and to endeavour to estimate their lasting value.[3]

A sad result of the lack of interest which previous generations had shown in the work of Galdós is the lack of good editions of his works. Not until C. A. Jones's discovery in 1959 was it realised that the novel *Doña Perfecta* exists in more than one version. The first, dated April 1876, was published in serial form in the *Revista de España* from March to May, thus clearly indicating that the novel was

---

[2]In *Luces de Bohemia, Opera omnia,* vol. XIX (Madrid, 1924), 82.

[3]An important exception to this generalisation is the interesting essay by Salvador de Madariaga in *The Genius of Spain* (Oxford, 1923). For a brief account of the revival of interest in Galdós, see "Galdós in the Light of of Recent Criticism", in *Galdós Studies,* ed. J. E. Varey (London, 1970), 1-35.

not finished when publication began. 1876 saw also two editions of the novel in book form, the first being published in June by the firm of Noguera (and later taken over by Bailly-Baillière); this closely follows the serialised version. The second edition in book form appeared later in the same year, being published by La Guirnalda, and here we find important changes, particularly affecting the end of the novel. It is this version which has been reprinted in such modern editions as the *Obras completas* edited by Federico Carlos Sainz de Robles and published by Aguilar. Jones points out that the most significant changes come in the letters at the end of the novel written by one of the characters, don Cayetano Polentinos, to an unnamed friend in Madrid. The first version presents a highly melodramatic ending, which clearly proved unacceptable to Galdós himself, and which, it has been argued, may have been the result of the pressure of publication. No doubt influenced by the reactions of critics and friends, Galdós rewrote the ending and his second version shows, as Jones points out, a movement towards the broad-minded tolerance which was later to typify his work. The novel in its new form, says the critic,

> could be interpreted as a plea for moderation on the part of both the conservative and the progressive, despite the survival of the cryptic final chapter. Certainly the later version gives evidence of very much better taste, and of a greater artistic sense (9, 573).

The artistic significance of the changes will be discussed later.

Doña Perfecta is, then, a novel which reflects the political and ideological struggles of its day: to use a modern phrase, it can be described as "littérature engagée". At the same time, it is the product of a young writer who is still endeavouring to find his own style, not completely sure of himself, and yet a work which foreshadows in many respects the great novels of Galdós's mature period.

II

The Opening Chapters

La Fontana de Oro (1867-1868) had been set in the period
1820-1823, *El audaz* (1871) in 1804, and the first series of the
Episodios nacionales (1873-1875) had dealt with historical events
covering the years 1805-1812. *Doña Perfecta* is set in the immediate
past, and begins with a train —that symbol of nineteenth-century
progress— awakening the sleeping countryside. The cocks are crowing
as a passenger descends into the cold dawn at the little way-side halt
of Villahorrenda. He is a young civil engineer, an *ingeniero de caminos*
come from Madrid to investigate the mineral deposits of the valley of
the Nahara and, in all probability, to marry his cousin, Rosario, who
lives with her mother in the city of Orbajosa. He is met by a sly-
looking peasant, Pedro Lucas or *el tío Licurgo,* and they prepare to
continue the journey on horseback. The train slowly pulls out of the
station and disappears whistling into a tunnel:

> El túnel, echando por su negra boca un hálito blanquecino,
> clamoreaba como una trompeta; al oír su enorme voz, despertaban
> aldeas, villas, ciudades, provincias. Aquí cantaba un gallo, más
> allá otro. Principiaba a amanecer (I; 416).

The opening of the novel suggests therefore the awakening of
Spain: the symbol of progress heralds the symbolic dawn. But as the
travellers move away from the way-side halt, they ride back into the
past, into the heart of Spain, as Chapter II is entitled. *El tío Licurgo*
gives the engineer, Pepe Rey, news of his aunt and of his cousin, and
of his aunt's brother, for ever shut in his library when not engaged in
archaeological pursuits. Rosario is anxiously awaiting the arrival of
Pepe: "la prima verá al primo, y todo será fiesta y gloria" (II; 417).
But a new note now creeps into the narration. The bridge is broken
and they will have to cross the river by the ford near the Cerrillo de

los Lirios. The young engineer is moved to sarcasm by the obvious contrast between the poetic names of the hills and valleys through which he is travelling, and the sorry reality: " ¡Cómo abundan los nombres poéticos en estos sitios tan feos! " (II; 417), he comments. A desolate plain is called Valleameno, a miserable village built of sun-baked bricks bears the proud title of Villarrica. There is a clear contrast, in the eyes of the traveller, between reality and nomenclature. Only Villahorrenda is aptly named. When he comes to his own lands, the treeless Alamillos de Bustamante, he again stresses the difference between the poetic description which his mother had given him of his inheritance, and the sad reality. Perhaps when he was young he too would have seen these lands with other eyes, but now he appreciates their true worth, and sees their "desolación miserable y perezosa" (II; 417). He also recalls that the owners of the surrounding lands have been gradually extending their boundaries and encroaching on his inheritance; for private property to be decently established, it is necessary that clear-cut boundaries should be agreed upon, he argues. *El tío Licurgo* informs him that *el tío Pasolargo*, known also as *el Filósofo*, has been guilty of encroaching on Pepe's lands, but it soon becomes apparent that he himself is not exempt from this reproach. The only well-farmed land in the vicinity turns out to belong to *el tío Licurgo* himself, but the farmer puts on a sad face as he gives the information. Pepe asks his pardon for thinking that the land belonged to him, and remarks that in this region "philosophy" is contagious. The sun is now rising, and the desolate countryside is fully revealed. With its splashes of colour, yellow, grey and dun, it looks like a patched and thread-bare garment, "semejaba en cierto modo a la capa del harapiento que se pone al sol" (II; 418), a comparison which would have pleased Antonio Machado, the poet who was to symbolise Castile as a beggar wrapped in rags. Just as Machado contrasts the sorry present with the warrior past of Castile, so Galdós reveals to us in these lands, as we look at them through the eyes of Pepe Rey, the historical past. Over these lands Christian and Moor had fought epic battles, "pero los combates de antaño los habían dejado horribles" (II; 418).

At this moment, shots are heard in the distance. Bandits are abroad, and, whilst *el tío Licurgo* counsels prudence, Pepe is ready to ride towards the shots in case he can be of assistance to any travellers that may have been attacked. This is a land of banditry, where robbers take to the hills and descend periodically to terrorise villages or rob and kill lonely travellers. But the appearance of a heavy wagon from the same direction suggests that the danger cannot be great, and they are informed by the carters that the shots they have heard did not betoken a bandit attack. The Civil Guard, charged with conveying half a dozen prisoners to gaol, has shot them en route. The smoke from the discharges can be seen rising in the air not far away. *El tío Licurgo* praises the Civil Guard for thus despatching a few good-for-nothings, who would probably have got off with comparatively light sentences and returned eventually to their old haunts. Much better that they should be shot according to the *ley de fuga;* that is to say, whilst, even though chained together, they are technically making a bid for freedom. "Lo mejor es esto: ¡fuego!, y adivina quién te dio" (II; 419). The spot at which the illegal and brutal execution took place is called, ironically, Las Delicias, and is also a favourite hide-out of the bandits.

The travellers are then overtaken by an energetic horseman, aptly nick-named *Caballuco,* a tough hard countryman:

> Volvióse nuestro viajero y vio un hombre, mejor dicho, un centauro, pues no podía concebirse más perfecta armonía entre caballo y jinete, el cual era de complexión recia y sanguínea, ojos grandes, ardientes, cabeza ruda, negros bigotes, mediana edad y el aspecto, en general, brusco y provocativo, con indicios de fuerza en toda su persona (II; 419).

He is carrying the mail to Orbajosa, and he salutes Pepe Rey politely enough, but with a certain arrogance:

hizo sus urbanidades con una expresión de altanería y superioridad
que revelaba, cuando menos, la conciencia de un gran valer o de
una alta posición en la comarca (II; 420).

When Pepe Rey asks *el tío Licurgo* who the horseman is, the latter is
surprised that in Madrid Pepe has not heard of the exploits and fame
of *Caballuco*. He is the local *cacique* —or political boss— and can
command the loyalty of all the brave fellows of the vicinity; he is kind
to the poor and a passionate upholder of the rights of Orbajosa and its
inhabitants. He is the son and grandson of men who had fought in
the *facción* —that is, who had taken part in the struggle against the
French and in the brutal civil wars of the early part of the century—
and it may well be that he in his turn will lead the *facción* in the
field since, according to *el tío Licurgo,* there is something rotten in
the state of present-day Spain, "todo está torcido y revuelto" (II;
420). *Caballuco* has heard from the Provincial Governor that troops
may be sent to this district and Pepe Rey concurs, saying that he had
heard this talked of in Madrid and that it would be well to prevent
the outbreak of further troubles. But *Caballuco* reacts strongly
against the idea of sending troops to Orbajosa. Madrid is a den of
thieves, he remarks, and if there is no *facción* in the field, then it is
high time that there were. He spurs his horse and rides on.

Half-an-hour later, the travellers arrive within sight of Orbajosa,
a city sprawled across a hill, its ruined city walls and tumbledown
castle standing out against the sky:

Un amasijo de paredes deformes, de casuchas de tierra pardas y
polvorosas, como el suelo, formaba la base, con algunos fragmentos
de almenadas murallas, a cuyo amparo mil chozas humildes alza-
ban sus miserables frontispicios de adobes, semejantes a caras ané-
micas y hambrientas que pedían una limosna al pasajero (II; 421).

The city gives an impression of sadness and poverty, and from a
distance its houses look like so many beggars silently pleading for
alms. Below the city is a mean river, and the only note of life is
given by the green fields and gardens along its banks. As they draw
nearer, they see the inhabitants entering and leaving, some on horse-

back and some on foot, and this gives at least some appearance of vital strength, for the "aspecto arquitectónico era más bien de ruina y muerte que de prosperidad y vida" (II; 421). The city is full of beggars, and as the travellers approach the gates they hear the clanging of discordant bells. The whole appearance of the city —as it is called officially, for although it is in reality a large village with only 7324 inhabitants, it is the seat of a bishopric and of the local jurisdiction— suggests death; if once it was alive and merited its alleged original Latin name of *Urbs augusta*,[4] the august city, it now gives the appearance of a sepulchre in which the life of the inhabitants is entombed. Pepe Rey, however, shrugs away his first reactions; for him it will always be dear as the birth-place of his mother, and here too he is looking forward to his first meeting with his aunt and with Rosario.

They enter the city, and see the house of doña Perfecta, the most important in the city, with five balconies giving on the Calle del Condestable and, behind the house, a garden. The gate of the garden is locked, but by standing on his stirrups, Pepe Rey can see his cousin through the trees. Beside her is a priest. As *el tío Licurgo* shouts the news of his arrival, Rosario leaves the side of the priest and runs towards the house. Pepe is attracted by her beauty, and by her blushes.

The first two chapters of the novel, then, give an apparently realistic picture drawn by an impartial narrator. The reader is aware, however, that he is in fact seeing the picture largely through the eyes of Pepe Rey. It is a series of ironic contrasts. As the travellers ride away from the railway and towards Orbajosa, they are riding into the past, into a land of ironies, where the very names suggest the opposite of the realities to which they are applied. It is a land stained by the

---

[4]It is don Inocencio, the priest, who puts forward this very doubtful etymon. Others prefer to derive the name of the city from *ajo* (garlic), the staple crop of the region (see below, p. 47).

blood of centuries of battle; nowadays the epic struggles of the past are reduced to banditry and unlawful executions, but nevertheless blood still stains the soil. It is a violent land, a land of death. The enthusiasm of the boy who accompanies the travellers when he hears the shots, and his disappointment when he is unable to see the bodies of the prisoners, suggests that death has become the main preoccupation of this desolate region. It is a land, too, of sly cunning, of quarrels among small landed proprietors, of law-suits and litigation, disputed boundaries and slow, tenacious avarice. The sun rises, but it reveals, not the new era to which Pepe looks forward and for which he is striving, but the decaying past. The tough *Caballuco* signifies the brutality of the region, and *el tío Licurgo*'s surprise that this local hero is not known in Madrid underlines the parochialism of the people. They are living in the past, unconscious of the ironies which surround them. But piercing the gloom are some rays of hope: the train whistle, the sun itself, the beauty and animation of Rosario, the green fields by the river. The scene is set for the meeting of the young people, but nevertheless the ironies of the first two chapters cannot fail to have impressed the reader. The smoke of the train finds a sinister counterpart in the smoke from the barrels of the Civil Guard's weapons; the light of the sun finds a contrast in the dark, sombre colours of the town. And Rosario is first seen beside *el señor Penitenciario,* the priest, although when she hears of the approach of the travellers she runs away from him towards the house.

In Chapter IV we meet the *señor Penitenciario,* don Inocencio Tinieblas, a life-long friend of the family, who, apart from his clerical duties as a Canon of the cathedral, had taught Latin and rhetoric in the school:

> Era un santo varón, piadoso y de no común saber, de intachables costumbres clericales, algo más de sexagenario, de afable trato, fino y comedido, gran repartidor de consejos y advertencias a hombres y mujeres (IV; 425).

This description betrays no irony on the part of the author. But we remark that, as Rosario leaves him and runs to her cousin he says to himself: "Vamos a conocer a ese prodigio" (IV; 425), suggesting that he has already made up his mind about Pepe's qualities and that he is by no means convinced that he is an ideal match for Rosario. The engineer is given a warm reception by his aunt, who can hardly speak for her emotion, which is evidently sincere. Rosario is introduced as a somewhat pale and delicate girl, her skin almost transparent. She is all "dulzura y modestia", and the novelist's description suggests that she lacks as yet a driving force in her life: "Allí faltaba materia para que la persona fuese completa: faltaba cauce, faltaban orillas" (IV; 425). She blushes violently when she is introduced to Pepe, and when she takes him to the room which has been prepared for him, it is clear that she has seen to all his wants with loving care. One window of his room looks on the cathedral, and the other over the garden. Rosario advises him not to keep them both open at once, "porque las corrientes de aire son muy malas" (IV; 426). Pepe is delighted with his cousin and with his reception; he tips *el tío Licurgo* handsomely, but again an uneasy note is struck when the latter reveals that he has initiated a law-suit against Pepe. As Pepe breakfasts, his aunt comments on the physical resemblance between father and son. She tells him that she has already revealed to Rosario her fears that, as a man used to the pomp and circumstance of life in Madrid and who has also lived in foreign countries, Pepe will find the life they lead in Orbajosa somewhat rustic and lacking in "buen tono" (V; 427). Pepe replies that he rejects the superficialities of so-called high society, and that recently he has often felt the impulse to rest from his studies and his labours and seek peace and tranquillity in the country:

> Crean ustedes que hace tiempo deseo darme, como decía no sé quién, un baño de cuerpo entero en la Naturaleza; vivir lejos del bullicio, en la soledad y sosiego del campo. Anhelo la tranquilidad de una vida sin luchas, sin afanes, ni envidioso ni envidiado, como dijo el poeta. Durante mucho tiempo, mis estudios, primero, y mis trabajos, después, me han impedido el descanso que necesito y

que reclaman mi espíritu y mi cuerpo; pero desde que entré en
esta casa, querida tía, querida prima, me he sentido rodeado de la
atmósfera de paz que deseo (V; 427).

The tone of the encounter so far is indeed one of love and harmony,
but, as Pepe speaks, the Canon, don Inocencio, makes his appearance:

Esto decía, cuando los cristales de la puerta que comunicaba el
comedor con la huerta se obscurecieron por la superposición de
una larga opacidad negra (V; 427).

The priest and Pepe Rey are introduced to each other, and don
Inocencio asks the engineer what impression he has formed of Orbajosa.
Pepe answers frankly —somewhat too frankly, indeed— that it is
evident to him that Orbajosa needs a new injection of capital, and
intelligent development of its resources. He stresses the number of
beggars to be seen in the streets, to which don Inocencio replies that
charity exists in order to look after such miserable wretches. The
town, he says, is far from being "un pueblo miserable" (IV; 428),
and doña Perfecta upholds him, claiming that Orbajosa produces
great crops of garlic although, as she explains, in recent years the
crops have suffered from lack of rainfall. Don Inocencio continues
in the same vein, rejecting the suggestion that new methods of
farming —English ploughs, seed drills, dams— and new methods of
finance are desirable. His words are full of bitter irony and sarcasm
as he speaks of the "hombres de tanto, de tantísmo talento" (IV; 428)
who come from the capital and despise the humility of the people of
Orbajosa. Pepe refrains from answering the priest in the same tone,
and tries to steer the conversation into non-controversial channels.
We then meet don Cayetano Polentinos, the brother of doña Perfecta.
He has collected a vast and important library, and his first words
concern the books which Pepe has brought him from Madrid, and he
clearly expects Pepe to be as passionately interested as he is himself
in matters of local erudition.

As they lunch, don Inocencio suggests to Pepe that he visit the
Cathedral, although he professes that "para hombres de tanto saber

como usted, quizás no tenga ningún mérito, y cualquier mercado de hierro será más bello" (VI; 430). The ironic tone of the priest, and his evident desire to provoke Pepe, are not lost on the engineer, but again he endeavours to keep his reactions to himself. Doña Perfecta warns him, laughingly, that she will be extremely angry with him if he does not find the Cathedral to be the eighth wonder of the world, and Pepe assures her that, from what he has seen of the exterior, he considers it to be a building of considerable architectural beauty. The Canon, however, continues his provocation and, insisting that Pepe must be considered as one of the outstanding figures of the day, he goes on to attack modern science as "la muerte del sentimiento y de las dulces ilusiones" (VI; 430). Science is the enemy of the arts, as it is the enemy of religion, caring for nothing which cannot be expressed in mathematical terms:

> Los admirables sueños del alma, su arrobamiento místico, la inspiración misma de los poetas, mentira. El corazón es una esponja; el cerebro, una gusanera (VI; 430).

Science is concerned only with machines:

> — Vamos, ¿me negará el señor don José —añadió el sacerdote— que la Ciencia, tal como se enseña y se propaga hoy, va derecha a hacer del mundo y del género humano una gran máquina? (VI; 430).

All burst into laughter, don Cayetano answers vaguely that there are two sides to every question and doña Perfecta offers the Canon more salad, adding that she knows he likes mustard. Clearly there is plenty of fire in his attack, and he finally provokes Pepe into a defence of science, even though he himself is not habitually accustomed to express his view of life, particularly at table and before the ladies. But such is the provocation of the Canon, that

> decidió manifestar las opiniones que más contrariaran y más acerbamente mortificasen al mordaz penitenciario. "Quieres divertirte conmigo —dijo para sí—. Verás qué mal rato te voy a dar" (VI; 430).

He praises science for having dealt the death-blow to superstition, "las mil mentiras de lo pasado", the world of illusions, of mysticism and false standards of art. The world is waking up and seeing clearly for the first time. "La fantasía, la terrible loca, que era el ama de la casa, pasa a ser criada." The fables of the past have been revealed for what they are: the only Mercury is Manzanedo; Mars is reduced to the figure of von Moltke, the German general; Nestor is Thiers, first minister of France, economist and historian; Orpheus is Verdi; Vulcan is Krupp, the German armaments manufacturer; Apollo is any modern poet. The myths of the past are dead, whether those of "paganismo, o idealismo cristiano". The only miracles are those which the scientist can perform in his laboratory, and of which he knows the rules and mysteries.

> En suma, señor Canónigo del alma, se han corrido las órdenes para dejar cesantes a todos los absurdos, falsedades, ilusiones, ensueños, sensiblerías y preocupaciones que ofuscan el entendimiento del hombre. Celebremos el suceso (VI; 430-431).

All this is said, as he reveals in an undertone to Rosario, with his tongue in his cheek, and merely to annoy the Canon, but the effect of Pepe's philippic on doña Perfecta is no less noticeable than on don Inocencio: she turns pale and looks significantly at the Canon.

The Canon pretends that it is hopeless for him to endeavour to refute the observations of such an intelligent and talented person as Pepe. But his argument is intended to suggest that true religion is opposed to Pepe's view of the world. Pepe breaks into laughter and confesses that his intention was to be provocative, and that in truth there is probably little difference between their viewpoints. But the Canon refuses to believe that Pepe was not presenting his own point of view: "No podía ser de otra manera. Usted es el hombre del siglo" (VII; 432). The mock-modest way in which he gives ground before the lofty intelligence of Pepe is seen by doña Perfecta as modesty and Christian charity. Pepe now realises that his provocative statements have put him in a difficult position, have led him into a labyrinth from which there is no easy escape. When don Cayetano turns the conversation to the subject of his archaeological discoveries, the Canon insists, despite Pepe's disavowals, that the engineer must also be an expert in the field, and doña Perfecta comments with evident sarcasm that nowadays "las universidades y las academias les instruyen de todo en un periquete, dándoles patente de sabiduría" (VII; 432). The Canon professes to believe that Pepe's true interests are in disputation, and suggests that he become a lawyer, provoking yet another philippic from Pepe, who attacks the standing of the profession and sees in it the cause of the enormous amount of litigation which is a curse of modern Spain:

> La primera y más terrible plaga de España es la turbamulta de jóvenes letrados, para cuya existencia es necesaria una fabulosa cantidad de pleitos (VII; 433).

Once again he is proved rash, for he does not know that don Inocencio's great-nephew, Jacinto, who has just graduated as a Doctor of Law, is considered to be a great legal luminary of the future, a true prodigy. Whilst Pepe stresses that he is speaking in generalities, his attack is nevertheless taken to be personal, and don Inocencio, whilst with mock humility accepting that Pepe may be correct, insinuates at the same time that Jacinto "no conoce sofisterías ni palabras huecas" (VII; 433). The Cathedral bell calls the canons to their office, and don Inocencio takes his leave, assuming an air of cordiality towards Pepe, but the engineer is only too relieved to see him withdraw. "La idea de que, sin quererlo, estaba en contradicción con las ideas de los amigos de su tía le mortificaba" (VII; 433). The meal which had begun in such good humour has ended on a bitter note.

III

Motives and Attitudes

My somewhat lengthy analysis of the opening of the novel, and in particular of the scene of the meal, has been necessary in order to show the gradual worsening of the relationships between the participants. Let us now examine the motives and attitudes which lay behind the superficial contest of words. Pepe Rey, as an engineer principally concerned with railways and with roads, knew provincial Spain. He had, for instance, worked on the railway which joined Tarragona and Montblanch, and he designed a bridge over the River Francolí. In 1870, after several years of working for construction firms, he had travelled abroad to Germany and England:

> Hombre de elevadas ideas y de inmenso amor a la Ciencia, hallaba su más puro goce en la observación y estudio de los prodigios con que el genio del siglo sabe cooperar a la cultura y bienestar físico y perfeccionamiento moral del hombre (III; 423).

A mature man, thirty-four years of age when he visited Orbajosa, well-built and tall, intelligent and possessing a strong will, he was also endowed with the capacity to get on with others and to earn their esteem and respect:

> Su persona bien podía pasar por un hermoso acabado símbolo, y si fuera estatua, el escultor habría grabado en el pedestal estas palabras: *inteligencia, fuerza* (III; 424).

Eloquent in private conversation, he was not usually given to moralising on the great topics of the day, but at the same time he hated falsehood. He was driven to attack all shams and superstitions, employing a mocking sarcasm which those whose views differed from his own tended to find shocking:

> No admitía falsedades ni mistificaciones, ni esos retruécanos del pensamiento con que se divierten algunas inteligencias impregnadas del gongorismo; y para volver por los fueros de la realidad, Pepe Rey

solía emplear a veces, no siempre con comedimiento, las armas de la burla. Esto casi era un defecto a los ojos de gran número de personas que le estimaban, porque aparecía un poco irrespetuoso en presencia de multitud de hechos comunes en el mundo y admitidos por todos (III; 424).

He was thus somewhat insensitive to the feelings of others, and the sad effects of this tendency are evident enough in the scene just described.

Nevertheless, despite his passion for the truth, we should also bear in mind that Pepe Rey did not come to Orbajosa without a pre-conceived idea of what he would find. His father, doña Perfecta's brother, had rescued the family's finances from the very parlous state in which they were left on the death of his spendthrift brother-in-law, and thus earned the genuine and undying gratitude of his sister. Gradually the idea had grown up that the two young cousins should marry and when, on Pepe's return from his journey abroad, his father announced to him that the dearest desire of his old age was to see the two branches of the family united, Pepe was not unwilling to enter-tain this project, although showing no great enthusiasm. It was for that reason that he had sought the commission to explore the mineral resources of the valley of the Nahara, in which Orbajosa lay; his professional activities would give a sense of purpose to his visit.

At the same time, and while being aware of the state of Spanish provinces from direct experience, he entertained other views of Orbajosa, views which derived from his mother's descriptions of her birthplace —as he told *el tío Licurgo*— and which were reinforced by his father's encomium of the tranquillity of life in the country:

— Por cierto —decía don Juan— que en esa remota Orbajosa, donde, entre paréntesis, tienes fincas que puedes examinar ahora, se pasa la vida con la tranquilidad y dulzura de un idilio. ¡Qué patriarcales costumbres!   ¡Qué nobleza en aquella sencillez! ¡Qué rústica paz virgiliana!   Si en vez de ser matemático fuera latinista, repetirías, al entrar allí, el *ergo tua rura manebunt.* ¡Qué admirable lugar para dedicarse a la contemplación de nuestra propia alma y prepararse a las buenas obras!   Allí todo es bondad, honradez; allí no se conocen la mentira y la farsa como en nuestras grandes ciudades; allí renacen las santas inclinaciones que el bullicio de la moderna vida ahoga; allí despierta la dormida fe, y se siente vivo impulso indefinible dentro del pecho, al modo de pueril impaciencia que en el fondo de nuestra alma grita: "Quiero vivir" (III; 423-424).

This picture of a Virgilian retreat, of a life of calm tranquillity, is clearly still in Pepe's mind when he reaches Orbajosa, and he makes definite reference to it whilst he breakfasts with his aunt, telling her that he feels himself "rodeado de la atmósfera de paz que deseo" (V; 427). But the myth of rustic tranquillity has already received some rude shocks: the brutal killing of the prisoners by the Civil Guard, the tales of banditry, the menace of law-suits, the ironic contrast between the poetic names and the sad realities of the countryside. Determined to find tranquillity in his aunt's home, and already attracted by the beauty of Rosario, Pepe endeavours to put these ideas behind him. He prefers the Virgilian myth to the crude reality which he has witnessed and on which he has commented: there is a rift between the poetic ideal and "reality" as he sees it.

Similarly, don Inocencio has also constructed his myth: but his is a destructive vision of the lamentable views of the "hombre del siglo". Pepe, by his definition, must be vain and conceited; he must think himself better than all the inhabitants of Orbajosa; he must have no respect whatsoever for religion; and he must have come with the intention of scorning the values by which Orbajosa supposedly lives. Pepe must necessarily also be a true representative of Madrid, which the *orbajosenses* conceive of as a den of thieves, ever ready to deny religion and all moral values, set on the destruction of those traditions which the *orbajosenses* hold most dear. Now, whilst this myth might explain why don Inocencio sarcastically calls Pepe a "prodigy" before he has ever set eyes on him, it does not explain why from the first he sets out to provoke the engineer into retaliation, until he is finally successful in making him state views which —although they

may not be held sincerely by Pepe, being intended rather to provoke
don Inocencio in his turn— serve to convince the Canon that his
diagnosis of Pepe was indeed correct. The author in fact does not
reveal until later in the novel that don Inocencio had a motive for his
actions. It had been for some time the dearly-loved hope of his
niece, Jacinto's mother, that one day the young legal luminary should
marry Rosario. There is therefore a double motivation behind
don Inocencio's attack, and perhaps Galdós has not played quite fair
with his readers, for the implication of the scene just described is
that the Canon is motivated only by a fundamental disagreement with
what he assumes will be Pepe's view of life.

Don Inocencio also cherishes another myth, one which is shared
by doña Perfecta, don Cayetano and Rosario: the myth of rustic
tranquillity and innocence, of plain living and high thinking. As
doña Perfecta welcomes Pepe, she tells him she fears he may be
bored by the slow life of the provincial city, and that he will find
them lacking in *bon ton*. Rosario, too, shares the same fears. But
whilst they are willing to believe that the life they lead may suffer
by comparison with the high life of Madrid —which, as it happens,
Pepe despises— they are nevertheless convinced of the sound moral
qualities of life in the country. Don Inocencio quotes Virgil and
suggests that one is nearer to God in the country than in the false
and superficial life of the capital.[5] He genuinely believes, as does
doña Perfecta, that Orbajosa does not lack for wealth and that the
garlic crop is of immense importance, despite the poor yields of
recent years. The inhabitants of Orbajosa, as we later discover, all

---

[5]Stephen Gilman links don Inocencio's use of classical tags with the appli-
cation of classical names (Lycurgus, the centaur) to characters in the novel
who embody a debased version of the original quality; "Las referencias
clásicas de *Doña Perfecta*", *Nueva Revista de Filología Hispánica*, III (1949),
353-362. Gustavo Correa sees the classical references as a symptom of the
debasement of previously-held ideals: "Lo característico . . . del mundo
cerrado de Orbajosa es el haber sufrido una deformación en sus esencias
culturales a través de los siglos"; *El simbolismo religioso en las novelas de
Pérez Galdós* (Madrid, 1962), 42.

cling fast to such beliefs, and all hold Madrid in abhorrence. Their inability to see the true nature of "reality" springs from a lack of standards, an ignorance of what the rest of the world is like. Pepe's myth of Orbajosa —before he sees it— is compounded of the sentimental pictures drawn by his mother and his father, and by the confusion of this sentimental picture with a literary commonplace. Just as don Inocencio quotes Horace, so Pepe quotes Fray Luis de León, and he tells his aunt that he longs, at times, like the sixteenth-century poet, to retire from the world and to live in rustic tranquillity, "ni envidioso, ni envidiado". (It is ironical that he slightly misquotes, and that he cannot remember the author of the other tag which springs to his lips.)

The danger of such attitudes is apparent. Pepe's professional eye cannot fail to see the lack of material resources in a city such as Orbajosa and the need for improvements. The poetic description is found to be false, although he endeavours to cling to his myth, seeing it now in terms of a moral retreat from the madding crowd. His travels and his experience have enabled him to see the gap which exists between myth and "reality". But the inhabitants of Orbajosa have no, or little, knowledge of the outside world, and their myth is impervious to criticism. It is clear that Galdós suggests, from the first encounter between Pepe Rey and his aunt and cousin, before the arrival of don Inocencio, that, despite their differing outlooks, it would have been possible for a harmonious personal relationship to be established. Doña Perfecta has a genuine sense of gratitude towards her brother, whom she sees reincarnated in his son; Rosario is already prejudiced in Pepe's favour; Pepe is already attracted to Rosario. But the dark shadow of don Inocencio falls upon them, and discord is sown. Subtly he provokes Pepe into an exaggerated statement of his outlook; foolishly, giving way to a weakness which we know already to exist, Pepe allows himself to be provoked and becomes in his turn provocative. Convinced that he is morally in the right, don Inocencio pursues his attack, and conveys clearly to doña Perfecta and to Rosario his belief that Pepe is godless, an enemy of religion, a hollow iconoclast. As Pepe praises science for having abolished "superstition", doña Perfecta significantly pales, and, equally significantly, looks towards the Canon. She begins to suspect that Pepe is an enemy of the faith. The inhabitants of Orbajosa begin to close ranks against the intruder. Their myth holds good: Pepe, like all other *madrileños*, is an infidel, and Orbajosa is the seat of religion and morality. And they are to hold to their myth right to the bitter end of the novel. Pepe's myth is destroyed; he sees Orbajosa for what it is, or for what he takes it to be, for Galdós has yet to reveal to the reader what is the author's "true" version of the reality of Orbajosa. The nature of the authorial comment in Chapters I and II, however, suggests that we should not be misled by appearances, nor taken in by myths.

From this point there is no turning back. The mutual attraction between Pepe Rey and Rosario grows into love; doña Perfecta has become suspicious of Pepe's views on religion; the Canon is adamantly against the match, not only because of his personal interest in the matter, but because he genuinely believes Pepe to be impious, immoral and conceited. Attitudes have crystallised, and sides have been chosen.

IV

The Development of the Situation

After the unfortunate lunch, Rosario shows herself unperturbed by Pepe's words, and the cousins go off together to the garden, a scene which we are left to imagine for ourselves. On the next day, however, meeting again in the garden, Pepe declares his love for Rosario:

> Sé que te quiero; que eres la mujer que desde hace tiempo me está anunciando el corazón, diciéndome noche y día: "Ya viene, ya está cerca; que te quemas" (VIII; 436),

and Rosario replies in similar terms with a tender look towards her cousin: "Te quiero desde antes de conocerte" (VIII; 436). It is significant that the lovers should have found their love for each other, and declared it openly, in direct contact with nature, for it is a natural love, a Romantic idyll: "Caía la tarde, y una dulce sombra se extendía por la parte baja de la huerta, mientras el último rayo del sol poniente coronaba de resplandores las cimas de los árboles" (VIII; 436). But the idyll —a true idyll, and no literary reminiscence— is broken by the arrival of the Canon, who has come to present Jacinto to Pepe Rey.

Once again the Canon endeavours to provoke Pepe Rey, and Jacinto asks the engineer what his views are on Darwinism. These are pin-pricks, but when doña Perfecta joins the group, she admonishes Pepe for his thoughtless and irreverent conduct in the Cathedral. Pepe had gone to examine the architecture and paintings, but, according to local gossip, he had shown himself indifferent to the Mass and disturbed the reverent at their worship. Pepe attempts to laugh off the accusation, but it is clear that, as he himself says, he already has a bad reputation in Orbajosa. The Canon ostensibly

endeavours to pour oil on troubled waters, but appreciably adds to
the storm, provoking Pepe into an attack on the bad taste of many
of the paintings and of the religious images which he has seen in the
church. In particular he attacks the ridiculous vestments of the images
of the Virgin and Child, only to discover that this is the image most
venerated by the *orbajosenses,* and that his aunt and cousin are
responsible for the vestments.   Once again, he has been led into
making unnecessarily provocative statements.   Doña Perfecta is
furious, and returns to the house with the Canon; Rosario weeps, but
only says mildly to Pepe: "Pero ¡qué cosas tienes! . . ." (IX; 442).
But at that moment doña Perfecta shouts angrily from the house,
calling Rosario to her. The idyll has been short-lived, and henceforth
the lovers are to be kept apart.

At this point Jacinto reveals to Pepe Rey the enormous number
of law-suits which have been laid against him. At the evening *tertulia,*
Pepe meets the local celebrities, and finds them indeed boring, no
less boring than don Cayetano with his great work on the historical
past of Orbajosa and its distinguished offspring. The days go by.
Pepe goes to the Casino, and becomes acquainted with the social
customs of the inhabitants. Gossip begins to spread about him;
all are convinced that he looks down on the *orbajosenses,* and that
he is a penniless adventurer hoping to marry a wealthy heiress. His
troubles with the law-suits show no signs of ending, and indeed
increase; doña Perfecta, whose influence would have been sufficient
to settle matters once and for all, claims that she is powerless.
Desperate, bored, furious, he all but determines to leave "aquella
tenebrosa ciudad de pleitos, de antiguallas, de envidia y de maledi-
cencia" (XI; 448). He has received no letters from Madrid for some
time; clearly they are being detained. When a letter does reach him,
it is only to tell him that he has been officially dismissed from his
commission: strings have been pulled, and the result is a serious
professional setback. Doña Perfecta assures him that his enemy must

be in Madrid, "en aquel centro de corrupción, de envidia y rivalidades, no en este pacífico y sosegado rincón, donde todo es buena voluntad y concordia . . ." (XI; 449). Despite his conviction that his true enemies are to be found in Orbajosa, he is persuaded to stay. When he asks why Rosario is not to be seen, he is told that she is not well and has shut herself within her room.

A new theme is then introduced. Deprived of the company of Rosario, he goes to the Casino where he is bored. On his way back, he glimpses some young girls on a balcony, and runs into don Juan Tafetán, an oldish man who still has an eye for a pretty female. The latter introduces him to the three girls, whose surname is Troya.[6] They live alone, shunned by the respectable inhabitants of Orbajosa, because they are penniless orphans. Somehow they manage to live by the needle; they seldom go out, but nevertheless appear to lead a happy and carefree existence. They are very irreverent towards their fellow townspeople, inventing nick-names, throwing orange peel at them as they pass by, and pebbles at the windows of the neighbouring houses. Whilst Pepe is there, they break a window in the house next door, and hit one of the inhabitants. The house turns out to be that of the Canon; the person struck is don Inocencio himself. From an upstairs window, Jacinto can see that Pepe is with the girls. A further reason for discord has arisen, later much embroidered by gossip, particularly when one of the girls changes the gold coin which Pepe has left for them, moved by the contrast between their empty-headed gaiety and their miserable existence. Pepe decides once more to leave Orbajosa, and his aunt makes all the necessary arrangements with a gleam in her eye. Meanwhile *Caballuco* appears; it transpires that he is an admirer of one of the Troya girls, and he confronts

---

[6]Chapter XII is entitled "Aquí fue Troya", and, as Gilman has commented, the classical reference is obvious. "En esa casa viven en una especie de sitio perpetuo tres míseras muchachas huérfanas, las niñas de Troya, rodeadas de suspicacias y desprecios y rechazadas por sus vecinos"; *Nueva Revista de Filología Hispánica,* III (1949), 356.

Pepe, saying "¿Sabe usted quién soy yo?", but Pepe brusquely
rejects him, answering, "Sí. Ya sé que es usted un animal" (XV;
460). All is now ready for Pepe's departure. He has, however,
persuaded a servant to take a message to Rosario, who remains shut
in her room. The answer is short, written on the margin of a
newspaper: "Dicen que te vas. Yo me muero" (XV; 460). He is
convinced that she is being deliberately shut away from him and,
reassured that she loves him, he cancels his decision to depart, to the
great consternation of his aunt. Pepe confronts doña Perfecta, the
Canon and *Caballuco:*

> Doña Perfecta los miró como mira un general a sus queridos
> cuerpos de ejército. Después examinó el semblante medita-
> bundo y sereno de Pepe Rey, de aquel estratégico enemigo que
> se presentaba inopinadamente cuando se le creía en vergonzosa
> fuga.
>   ¡Ay!   ¡Sangre, ruina y desolación! . . . Una gran batalla se
> preparaba (XV; 460).

Battle lines are drawn up.

That night don Cayetano, whilst wearying Pepe with a further
account of his life's work, also tells the engineer that there is a taint
of hereditary madness in the female side of the family, a tendency
to mania, which he alone has escaped (a further irony, since he is
clearly somewhat unbalanced in his historical and archaeological
enthusiasms). Later, from the window of his room, Pepe sees a
handkerchief fluttering from Rosario's window, and a hand pointing
towards the lower part of the house. Stealing out of his room, he
meets his cousin and they are able to talk in the dark, in the private
chapel of the household, seated at the foot of the crucifix. Pepe
assures his cousin that he is indeed a believing Christian. Rosario
does not appear to be physically ill, but Pepe assures her that she is
suffering from a nervous affection, a "perturbación moral". He asks
her to have confidence in him, and she replies:

> Tus palabras resuenan en mi corazón como golpes violentos que,
> estremeciéndome, me dan nueva vida. Aquí, en esta obscuridad,

donde no podemos vernos las caras, una luz inefable sale de ti y
me inunda el alma. ¿Qué tienes tú, que así me transformas?
Cuando te conocí, de repente fui otra (XVII; 465).

They swear undying love for each other before Christ, and the
engineer resists the obvious temptation which the occasion offers.
They will be united, come what may.

As the next day dawns, a troop of soldiers marches into Orbajosa;
the government fears another rising in the provinces and this region
is famed for its intransigence. The coming of the troops appears at
first sight to be to the advantage of Pepe, particularly when he
discovers that one of the officers, billeted in doña Perfecta's house,
is an old friend, Pinzón. He conceives an audacious plan to carry off
Rosario from her aunt's house, and Pinzón, although not underrating
the difficulties, promises all possible help. But in fact the entry of
the troops brings with it violence, a violence mirrored in a stormy
scene between Pepe and his aunt in Chapter XIX which is entitled
"Combate terrible.—Estrategia". Pepe Rey insists that he will marry
Rosario against all opposition, and his aunt turns him from the house.
The government is showing further signs of concern, and the local
judge is replaced by one upon whom they can rely. As the government
increases its pressure, so attitudes harden in Orbajosa and the
inhabitants begin to react. *Caballuco* is finally persuaded by doña
Perfecta that he must break his word given previously to the Governor
of the province, and organise armed resistance. Taunted by doña
Perfecta, he at last gives way.

Meanwhile a servant has been suborned, and Rosario has been
visited, apparently by Pinzón, but, as doña Perfecta suspects, this
was in fact Pepe Rey disguised as his friend. Rosario confesses, alone
before God:

Señor, Dios mío, ¿por qué antes no sabía mentir y ahora sé?
¿Por qué antes no sabía disimular y ahora disimulo? ¿Soy una
mujer infame . . .? ¿Esto que siento y que a mí me pasa es la
caída de las que no vuelven a levantarse? ¿He dejado de ser

buena y honrada? . . . Yo no me conozco. ¿Soy la misma, o es otra la que está en este sitio? . . . ¡Qué de terribles cosas en tan pocos días! (XXIV; 487).

Torn between love for Pepe and respect for her mother, she at last brings herself to the awful admission: " ¡Señor, que aborrezco a mi madre!" (XXIV; 488).

Jacinto's mother, María Remedios, still hoping to marry her son to Rosario, suggests to the Canon that Pepe Rey be set upon in the street and given a "susto". Eventually the Canon is prevailed upon to order *Caballuco* to attack Pepe, and, although he symbolically washes his hands after giving the order, the guilt is clearly his. The "susto" becomes a murder. As Pepe Rey goes to meet Rosario in the garden of the house, he is seen by María Remedios and *Caballuco*. The latter follows Pepe into the garden, whilst María Remedios hammers on the front door and discloses what is happening. Doña Perfecta rushes to the door which leads to the garden, shouting "Cristóbal, Cristóbal . . ., ¡mátale! " (XXXI; 508). As *Caballuco* attacks Pepe with a knife, the engineer shoots at him, and misses. *Caballuco* does not miss.

The end of the story is told in a series of letters from don Cayetano in which, amid queries about the proofs of the great work, the pedant reveals to a friend in Madrid that Pepe is dead, that Rosario has been consigned to an asylum, that don Inocencio has gone on a pilgrimage to Rome, and that doña Perfecta has given herself up to the practice of her religion:

Gracias a ella, el culto ha recobrado en Orbajosa el esplendor de otros días. Esto no deja de ser un alivio en medio de la decadencia y acabamiento de nuestra nacionalidad . . . (XXXII; 511).

V

The Characters

Let us now consider the presentation of the characters and the parts they play in this melodramatic action. Pepe Rey is presented by the author in Chapter III as a typical "Victorian", if the expression may be permitted, "el hombre del siglo". From an early age he had shown an aptitude for mathematics, and he grows up to be a civil engineer. We are told little of his schooling, and we do not discover a great deal about his professional activities. His visit to Germany and to England is intended to demonstrate that he had been exposed to societies other than that of Spain, which Galdós shows in later novels —such as *La de Bringas*— to be still an enclosed society up to the time of the abdication of Isabel II in 1868. Pepe found his greatest pleasure, so the author tells us, in the observation and study of the prodigious feats of the nineteenth century in which the spirit of the age made its contribution to culture and to the physical betterment and moral improvement of mankind. We are not told, however, exactly what these prodigies were. Is Galdós referring to such material works as the new railway network, the development of heavy industries, the technological advances of the mid-nineteenth century? Pepe Rey, for all his professional quali-fications, does not give the impression of being a Brunel, and Galdós lost a significant opportunity when he failed to show us the engineer busy at his professional duties when he first arrives in Orbajosa. The development of mineral resources and the planning of a railway would have provided an ideal situation in which to develop the litigious tendencies of the small landowners of Orbajosa. We must conclude that, whilst Galdós wishes to make Pepe Rey into a symbol, he is not himself clear about exactly what the engineer is to symbolize.

Is it technical progress, or is it a new way of looking at the world? In Chapter III Galdós tells us that Pepe, a man of great intelligence, had a deep respect for the truth, and was an avowed enemy of shams and pretensions. He did not mince his words, and was apt to provoke his opponents. This latter characteristic is all too evident in the description of the lunch in Chapters V-VII. Here it is not clear exactly what the position of Pepe is, since he is being deliberately provocative. We can see, however, that behind the surface provocation, he respects science as an enemy of falsehood and superstition. In the dispute concerning his conduct in the Cathedral, he again shows himself to be concerned more with the deep meaning of religion than with its superficial characteristics. The Canon accuses him of being concerned with exteriors: "Pero, en fin, hoy es costumbre adorar la forma, no la idea" (IX; 440), whereas in fact this is the very point of view which Pepe is attacking: the bad taste of much popular religious art, the concern for outward appearance and show at the expense of true religion.

> — No puedo resistir —añadió Pepe— aquellas imágenes charoladas y bermellonadas, tan semejantes, perdóneme Dios la comparación, a las muñecas con que juegan las niñas grandecitas. ¿Qué puedo decir de los vestidos de teatro con que las cubren? (IX; 440).

Great religious works of art, however, can raise the soul to the contemplation of higher things:

> Las grandes obras de arte, dando formas sensibles a las ideas, a los dogmas, a la fe, a la exaltación mística, realizan misión muy noble (IX; 441).

Pepe is only to some extent puritanical, and even then he is a puritan within the Catholic tradition. He does not wish to bar all works of art of whatever nature from the churches; he merely wishes to see better art used for religious purposes: "Vivan las artes, despliéguese la mayor pompa en los ritos religiosos. Yo soy partidario de la pompa . . ." (IX; 441). His opponents classify such criticism of the externals of their religious observances with atheism and iconoclasm.

Galdós makes an evident contrast between the description of the sacred images in the Cathedral, and that of the crucifix in the family chapel. There the lovers meet in the darkness, recalling the persecuted Christians in the catacombs, and face God. Pepe shows himself to be a true believer; the light shines in the darkness, as the heading of Chapter XVII suggests. "Una luz inefable sale de ti y me inunda el alma" (XVII; 465), says Rosario. Their love unites the two cousins, and their love will triumph over all obstacles, since they feel their union to be blessed by God. Pepe, however, also feels less elevated emotions, but his carnal instincts are checked by the crucifix itself. As he clasps Rosario in his arms, his head strikes the feet of the crucified Christ, and he addresses the figure, saying: "Señor, no me pegues, que no haré nada malo" (XVII; 465). Rosario proclaims their love before Christ, and falls exhausted into Pepe's arms. Once again he is tempted:

> Por la mente del ingeniero pasó como un rayo la idea de que existía el Demonio; pero entonces el Demonio era él (XVII; 466).

But once again the temptation to avenge himself by seducing Rosario is resisted. When he first saw Rosario's beckoning arm he had been assaulted by mixed emotions:

> En su alma reinaba una ternura exaltada y profunda. Pero ¿a qué negarlo?, tras aquel dulce sentimiento surgió de repente, como infernal inspiración, otro que era un terrible deseo de venganza (XVI; 463).

But the implicit trust which Rosario has in him, and the proximity of the crucifix, are sufficient guide to his conscience. The frank avowals of their love are therefore expressed before a figure of Christ stripped of all external trappings: before a figure which represents the true essence of religion, and not its outward form. But their love is doomed.

As the storm gathers, Pepe prefers the tactics of the oak to those of the reed. After the scene in which he is chided for his conduct in the Cathedral, he is furious, furious with himself and with the persons

with whom he has quarrelled, as he endeavours to "indagar la causa
de aquella pugna, entablada a pesar suyo entre su pensamiento y el
pensamiento de los amigos de su tía" (X; 442). But he cannot submit;
he cannot bring himself to compromise with the society of Orbajosa:

> Era su carácter nada maleable, duro y de muy escasa flexibilidad,
> y rechazaba las perfidias y acomodamientos de lenguaje para
> simular la concordia cuando no existía (X; 444).

His stubbornness extends to his attitude to the legal traps which are
laid for him : "Su honra estaba comprometida, y no había otro
remedio que pleitear o morir" (XI; 447). Here we can see how the
myth of the tranquil life of the country has been resolved, as far as
the engineer is concerned. Pepe Rey now sees Orbajosa in terms of
black and white. No compromise is possible. No longer does reason
govern him, but emotion: his love for Rosario, and his hatred of all
that Orbajosa comes to stand for in his eyes.

> Representábase en su imaginación a la noble ciudad de su madre
> como una horrible bestia que en él clavaba sus feroces uñas y le
> bebía la sangre. Para librarse de ella bastábale, según su creencia,
> la fuga; pero un interés profundo, como interés del corazón, le
> detenía, atándole a la peña de su martirio con lazos muy fuertes
> (XIV; 447).

His pity is invoked by the treatment meted out to the Troya girls;
his wrath is kindled by the Bishop's order that he be expelled from
the Cathedral. He still manages to control his temper, however:

> Pepe Rey se hallaba en esa situación de ánimo en que el hombre
> más prudente siente dentro de sí violentos ardores y una fuerza
> ciega y brutal que tiende a estrangular, abofetear, romper cráneos
> y machacar huesos. Pero doña Perfecta era señora y, además, su
> tía. Don Inocencio era anciano y sacerdote. Además de esto, las
> violencias de obra son de mal gusto, impropias de personas
> cristianas y bien educadas (XIV; 458).

But with the discovery that his cousin is locked in her room, and
that she still loves him, open warfare is declared.

Pepe Rey has come into contact with something greater than
himself, and a fundamental weakness is revealed:

Hombre de gran energía por lo común, cualquier accidente de sensibilidad, cualquier agente que obrase sobre su corazón, le trocaba de súbito en niño. Achaques de matemático. Dicen que Newton era también así (XIX; 472).

This quotation comes at the point where he is struck by the firmness of doña Perfecta's belief that she is in the right. But his aunt's firmness produces an equal and opposite reaction in the engineer:

`Doña Perfecta se levantó indignada, majestuosa, terrible. Su actitud era la del anatema hecho mujer. Rey permaneció sentado, sereno, valiente, con el valor pasivo de una creencia profunda y de una resolución inquebrantable (XIX; 473).

From now on there can be no compromise.

It is incorrect to say that there is no development in the character of Pepe Rey. We first see him enthusiastic, straightforward, friendly, even though a little precipitate and inconsiderate in his manner. But from now on he decides to fight his antagonists on their own terms, he begins to work underground, to plot and plan. His temper becomes frayed, and he himself fully recognises the change which has come over him. He is, and was, "manso, recto, honrado y enemigo de violencias", but faced with the martyrdom of Rosario, he becomes a changed man:

Este espectáculo, esta injusticia, esta violencia inaudita es la que convierte mi rectitud en barbarie, mi razón en fuerza, mi honradez en violencia parecida a la de los asesinos y ladrones . . . Era razonable, y soy un bruto; era respetuoso, y soy insolente; era culto, y me encuentro salvaje(XIX; 475).

The blame he lays at this stage on doña Perfecta herself. He has met an immovable object, and this has converted him into an irresistible force :

Hago lo que hacen las sociedades cuando una brutalidad, tan ilógica como irritante, se opone a su marcha. Pasan por encima, y todo lo destrozan con feroz acometida (XIX; 475).

The difference between *Caballuco* and Pepe Rey, so obvious and clear on that first meeting as the engineer rode towards Orbajosa, becomes blurred; if he taunts *Caballuco* with being no more than an animal, is he any better at the end of the novel? The plan to suborn the servant, the entrance into the house disguised as Pinzón, the seduction of Rosario —for so we must interpret her confession before God and her confession to her mother— all mark him down as having abandoned his ethical and moral standards. And shortly before his death he makes his own confession, in the letter written to his father:

> He cambiado mucho. Yo no conocía esos furores que me abrasan. Antes me reía de toda obra violenta, de las exageraciones de los hombres impetuosos, como de las brutalidades de los malvados. Ya nada de esto me asombra, porque en mi mismo encuentro a todas horas cierta capacidad terrible para la perversidad. A usted puedo hablarle como se habla a solas con Dios y con la conciencia; a usted puedo decirle que soy un miserable, porque es un miserable quien carece de aquella poderosa fuerza moral contra sí mismo que castiga las pasiones y somete la vida al duro régimen de la conciencia. He carecido de la entereza cristiana que contiene el espíritu del hombre ofendido en un hermoso estado de elevación sobre las ofensas que recibe y los enemigos que se las hacen; he tenido la debilidad de abandonarme a una ira loca, poniéndome al bajo nivel de mis detractores, devolviéndoles golpes iguales a los suyos y tratando de confundirlos por medios aprendidos en su propia indigna escuela (XXVIII; 501).

He has succumbed to his passions, to anger, the worst of all the human passions, for it can entirely change the character of a human being. If doña Perfecta's responsibility for what has occurred, and what might still occur, is immense, so is that of Pepe himself:

> Lo que más amarga mi vida es haber empleado la ficción, el engaño y bajos disimulos. ¡Yo, que era la verdad misma! He perdido mi propia hechura . . . (XXVIII; 502).

The mask of progress has been dropped, the dog beneath the skin revealed. Violence has engendered violence, and in the final reckoning there is no real difference between the progressive and the reactionary when both come under the sway of passion. Both are *facciosos* in their own cause: "Hemos venido a ser tan bárbaro el uno como el otro" (XIX; 475).

Rosario also shows some development of character, although the exigencies of the plot entail her virtual disappearance from the second half of the novel. As we have seen, she is a tender creature, emotional, loving, lacking in character largely because she has come up against no force which will determine her growth. Her emotional and spiritual life has been conditioned by her mother and by don Inocencio, and by the *ambiente* of Orbajosa itself. She feels a sense of pre-destination which draws her towards Pepe, and her love for him is sincere and deep. Once her mother comes to the conclusion that Pepe is an undesirable match for her daughter, she is forcibly locked away. Torn between love for Pepe and filial respect, she begins to wonder if in reality she is going mad, if the hereditary strain of insanity is declaring itself in her. But when she meets Pepe in the chapel she reveals that her love for him has indeed transformed her, and discovered in her a strength which hitherto she had not known she possessed:

> Haré lo que me dices: me levanto y te sigo. Iremos juntos a donde quieras. ¿Sabes que me siento bien? ¿Sabes que no tengo ya fiebre, que recobro las fuerzas, que quiero correr y gritar, que todo mi ser se renueva, y se aumenta y se centuplica para adorarte? (XVII; 465).

Her love is genuine and strong, and as she declares her passion before God she cries:

> Haz que el mundo no se oponga a nuestra felicidad, y concédeme el favor de esta unión, que ha de ser buena ante el mundo como lo es en mi conciencia (XVII; 465).

But the opposition of her mother and Pepe's decision to work under-ground produce a new situation; disguised as Pinzón, Pepe is able to pass into the house and to see Rosario secretly. What transpires is not related directly, but can be read between the lines of Rosario's confession to God:

> Soy más mala que las peores mujeres de la Tierra. Dentro de mí, una gran culebra me muerde y me envenena el corazón . . . (XXIV; 487).

Pure love has been sullied and tarnished. Rosario has to confess to herself that she now abhors her mother, even though her only wish is to love her:

> Quiero amar tan sólo. Yo no nací para este rencor que me está devorando. Yo no nací para disimular, ni para mentir, ni para engañar. Mañana saldré a la calle, gritaré en medio de ella, y a todo el que pase le diré: "Amo, aborrezco" . . . Mi corazón se desahogará de esta manera . . . ¡Qué dicha sería poder conciliarlo todo, amar y respetar a todo el mundo! (XXIV; 488).

A plan is laid for Pepe to abduct her, but, faced with her mother's passion, Rosario finds herself unable to keep back the truth. She unburdens herself, confessing that she has planned to go away with Pepe: "Hemos concertado casarnos. Es preciso, mamá, mamá mía querida" (XXXI; 507). "Es mi esposo" (XXXI; 507), cries Rosario, and it is at this moment that María Remedio arrives with the news that Pepe Rey has been seen in the garden. Rosario has suffered, and has grown in stature; her sentimental nature is not however strong enough to resist the forces which act upon her. Conscience-stricken, overcome by the news of Pepe's death, she goes mad, finally and irrevocably.

Don Inocencio also suffers a change during the course of the novel. A man of scrupulous conduct, kind and generous, he nevertheless allows his personal desires to colour his views of Pepe Rey, and it is this which urges him to make Pepe expose himself for what he believes him to be. He loses no opportunity to cast doubt on the suitability of Pepe as a husband for Rosario, and as the bitterness increases, he upholds doña Perfecta's decision to oppose the marriage at all costs. His great struggle comes in the scene in which María Remedios is urging him to order *Caballuco* to give Pepe "un susto". At first he resists her, saying that "jamás aconsejaré que se empleen medios violentos y brutales" (XXVII; 499). Whilst this may be literally true, he has nevertheless been present at the meeting in which doña Perfecta urges *Caballuco* to take to the country with his men, and to resist the government by force of arms. It is he who now asks *Caballuco* if he will that night accompany María Remedios, and he tells him that Pepe has insulted his niece. He still endeavours to maintain his attitude of not counselling violent means, but it is the Canon who insists, somewhat against *Caballuco*'s will, that the latter accompany María Remedios, and for all that he washes his hands after the affair, he is not able to wash out the stain of blood. At the end of the novel we learn, through don Cayetano, that since the sad events took place, the Canon has been "tan acongojado, tan melancólico, tan taciturno, que no se le conoce" (XXXII; 510). He has shut himself away from everyone, quarrelled with María Remedios, announced that he will resign his canonry and go on a pilgrimage to Rome. Whatever his faults, don Inocencio does not lack a conscience.

The change which takes place in doña Perfecta during the course of the novel appears at first sight most surprising; this is, however, a difference of attitude, rather than a development of character. After the opening scenes, in which we see her eagerly awaiting her nephew, pleased to be able to repay some of the kindness of her brother, hoping evidently for the match between Rosario and Pepe Rey to take place, her change of front appears at first sight very abrupt. But has she in fact changed basically? Formed by her upbringing in Orbajosa, and by her late husband's spendthrift life in Madrid, she genuinely believes that Orbajosa stands for peace, tranquillity and a high moral standard, and that Madrid is necessarily vicious and depraved. Her concern for religion is sincere, but is largely concerned with the outward manifestations of cult, rather than the depths of belief. Once she is convinced that Pepe is no fit husband for Rosario, she begins to work against him. Rosario is in love with Pepe, and she is forcibly kept apart from him. Strings are pulled in Madrid, letters are kept back, law-suits encouraged. Pepe's life becomes a misery. In the great confrontation which occurs in Chapter XIX, she shows that in her eyes it is proper to use underhand methods to achieve an end which is considered to be good. She confesses to Pepe that she had indeed employed subterfuges to achieve her object:

> Yo, querido sobrino, ostentando una sinceridad que tú no mereces, te confieso que sí, que efectivamente me he valido de subterfugios para conseguir un fin bueno, para conseguir lo que al mismo tiempo era beneficioso para ti y para mi hija . . . (XIX; 472).

But despite this avowal, she is firmly convinced that she is in the right:

> Yo soy una mujer piadosa, ¿entiendes? Yo tengo mi conciencia tranquila, ¿entiendes? Yo sé lo que hago y por qué lo hago, ¿entiendes? (XIX; 472-473).

Her very strength is her greatest defect. She sets herself up to judge and to condemn; she has decided for herself what is the true nature of Pepe Rey, and no arguments can prevail against her obstinate prejudices. She uses all weapons in her fight against Pepe, prevailing upon *Caballuco* to lead the *facción* into the field, playing upon his *hombría*, twisting him round her finger, perverting truth, making him break his word, and then pretending that her motive is not the defeat of Pepe's plans but the protection of innocent Orbajosa against the soldiery. In Chapter XXXI she is revealed as calmly seated at her writing-table, and the author informs us that her relations with well-placed friends in Madrid had enabled her to bring about the dismissal of Pepe Rey from his government commission. The author speaks of her "costumbres intachables", her "bondad pública", but, he reveals, this hides a narrow fanaticism and a lack of true charity:

> No sabemos cómo hubiera sido doña Perfecta amando. Aborreciendo, tenía la inflamada vehemencia de un ángel tutelar de la discordia entre los hombres. Tal es el resultado producido en un carácter duro y sin bondad nativa por la exaltación religiosa, cuando ésta, en vez de nutrirse de la conciencia y de la verdad revelada en principios tan sencillos como hermosos, busca su savia en fórmulas estrechas que sólo obedecen a intereses eclesiásticos (XXXI; 506).

The confession of her daughter only causes her anger to grow more intense; she shows little concern for Rosario's afflictions, and even when her daughter faints, doña Perfecta takes no notice, as she goes to confront Pepe Rey:

> Exploró doña Perfecta la obscuridad con sus ojos llenos de
> ira. El rencor les daba la singular videncia de la raza felina
> (XXXI; 507).

And it is she who gives the order for the killing of her nephew. At
the end of the novel, again through the eyes of don Cayetano, we see
her plunged in gloom, and consoling herself with the practice of the
outward forms of religion. Doña Perfecta has failed to learn from her
experiences, and, we are led to believe, is still convinced that she
acted for the best.

It is possible to agree to some extent with a critic such as Michael
Nimetz, when he writes:

> In *Doña Perfecta*, Galdós uses the techniques of caricature for
> symbolic purposes. His people are the embodiments of good and
> evil, progress and reaction, ignorance and enlightenment, and so on.

Nimetz argues that the distortions of the characters, attacked by
many critics, constitute one of the greatest assets of the novel:

> Galdós wanted to write a polemic and he did. Judged as such,
> *Doña Perfecta* is a powerful work (11, 144).

But whilst it is true that there is a strong element of caricature in the
minor characters, I have endeavoured to demonstrate that the major
characters do show some development in the course of the action.
Galdós did not intend them to appear wholly one-sided, and if they
do so, this is in part due to the inexperience of the novelist, and in
part due to the inbuilt prejudice of the reader.

VI

The Conflict: Social Criticism

The conflict in the novel can be defined in one sense as the new against the old: nineteenth-century progress versus the conservation of old traditions. Don Inocencio and doña Perfecta cling throughout the novel to the belief that all is well in Orbajosa, that here are to be found the true traditions of Spain and of Catholicism, that here all is sobriety, wisdom, high thinking and moral ideals. Their myth is shared at the beginning of the novel by Rosario and, as we have seen, influenced by his mother's childhood memories and his father's rosy-coloured visions, Pepe too holds to a version of this myth at the outset of his journey. Don Cayetano, a caricature of a pedantic provincial bookworm, is similarly convinced of the reality of the myth: "Los habitantes de Orbajosa bastan por sí solos para dar grandeza y honor a un reino" (X; 446). His might be called the historical projection of the myth, for he still lives in the past, surrounded by the glories of Spanish might in the sixteenth and seventeenth centuries, and only too happy when he discovers yet a further reference to an illustrious son of Orbajosa, even though his discovery is completely negative:

> He descubierto un nuevo orbajosense ilustre, Bernardo Amador de Soto, que fue espolique del duque de Osuna, le sirvió durante la época del virreinato de Nápoles, y aun hay indicios de que no hizo nada, absolutamente nada, en el complot contra Venecia (XXXII; 511).

According to his own account, he is the only one of his family who has escaped the hereditary mania. His love for the ivory tower is accentuated by his own selfish character: when the storm blows up, he prefers to weather it in the calm haven of his library, and his letters at the end of the novel cause us to lose all sympathy for him. His first concern is for a rare book for sale in an auction, and it is only later that he informs his correspondent that Pepe has been killed. He lacks a sense of proportion, and the bitterness with which Galdós presents the character robs him of any pretence of realism. Against doña Perfecta, don Inocencio and don Cayetano are set Pepe Rey and, to a lesser extent, Pinzón. Pinzón shows an evident distrust of local politicians, and is convinced that a new civil war is about to break out. He sees much more clearly than Pepe Rey the double standards of Orbajosa, and faces their machinations with open eyes. He is not, however, fully realised as a character. The conflict in the novel, then, is two-fold. Galdós presents not only the opposition between progress and conservatism rooted in obscurantism, but also the opposition between Madrid and the provinces. The conflict has social, moral and political aspects.

The first impression we are given of the social realities of Orbajosa is through the eyes of Pepe Rey. He sees the town as in need of material development. It is full of beggars, many of whom are "sanos y aun robustos" (V; 428), and his conclusion is that there is a need for an expansion of agriculture and industry. The cathedral is a fine building, the main street contains some imposing old houses, but the rest of the town consists of sorry modest dwellings. The interior of doña Perfecta's house is pleasant, or so Pepe sees it at first, still determined to cling to his idealised view. The living room is spacious, filled with light. The main ornaments are a clock, with a pendulum "diciendo perpetuamente que *no*" (V; 428), and the principal decorations are pictures of the exploits of Hernán Cortés seen through the deforming vision of a French artist. The other principal adornment is a parrot's cage, standing outside the door which leads to the garden. Don Inocencio is, perhaps significantly, fond of the parrot, with its "fisonomía irónica y dura", its "casaca verde" and "roncas palabras burlescas" (V; 428). The way in which he addresses it suggests that the Canon notes a similarity between the parrot and his view of the *madrileños*: "De charlatanes está lleno el mundo de los hombres y el

de los pájaros" (V; 429), but he himself parrots an out-of-date vision
of Orbajosa and repeats mechanically the provincial strictures on the
society of Madrid. This first description of the sun-filled room gives
way later in the novel, as tension increases, to darkness. The house
becomes the prison of Rosario, and the only light in the darkness
comes from their mutual avowal of love in the chapel. Orbajosa is
indeed a sad city. The only real life appears to be that of the Casino
and, when weather permits, that of the evening *paseo*, where the
"brillante pléyade" of the youth of Orbajosa walk up and down
between "dos hileras de tísicos olmos y algunas retamas descoloridas",
commenting on the young girls as they pass by (XI; 446). The
Casino in the evenings is no more animated; some play cards, others
read the newspapers, but most gossip. "El resumen de todos los
debates era siempre la supremacia de Orbajosa y de sus habitantes
sobre los demás pueblos y gentes de la Tierra" (XI; 446).

The inhabitants of Orbajosa show themselves entirely convinced of
the town's wealth and status. Doña Perfecta proudly tells her nephew
that Orbajosa produces the best garlic in Spain, and that there are
more than twenty rich families living in the town. She continues:

> Verdad es . . . que los últimos años han sido detestables a causa de
> la seca; pero, aun así, las paneras no están vacías, y se han llevado
> últimamente al mercado muchos miles de ristras de ajos (V; 428).

The gossipers in the Casino speak even more strongly in the same
vein; Orbajosa produces a great quantity of olive oil and corn:

> ¿No sabe ese estúpido que en años buenos Orbajosa da pan para
> toda España y aún para toda Europa? Verdad que ya llevamos no
> sé cuantos años de mala cosecha; pero eso no es ley. ¿Pues y la
> cosecha del ajo? ¿A que no sabe este señor que los ajos de
> Orbajosa dejaron bizcos a los señores del Jurado en la Exposición
> de Londres? (XI; 447).

The idea of Orbajosa contributing a display of garlic to the Great
Exhibition of 1851 is richly comic. The repeated motif of the praise
of Orbajosa's produce followed by the acknowledgement that crops
have not been good in recent years suggests that the town is living on

past glories, even in agriculture. The stress on the production of
garlic —"ajos"— suggests a further etymology for the name of the
town. Instead of being the *urbs augusta* of don Inocencio's etymology,
the name may perhaps suggest the *urbs ajosa,* that which produces
most garlic. Indeed, the myth of Orbajosa is typified in the first
etymology, and the view of the outsiders in the second. The Canon
is quite content with things as they are, and resists the introduction
of new machinery and new agricultural methods:

> Aquí estamos muy bien sin que los señores de la Corte nos visiten,
> mucho mejor sin oír ese continuo clamoreo de nuestra pobreza y
> de las grandezas y maravillas de otras partes (V; 428).

Like the other inhabitants, he does not want to hear of the rest of
the world. For the *orbajosenses,* theirs is a splendid city, able to
bear comparison with almost any European capital:

> ¿Dónde habrá visto él, como no sea en París, una calle semejante
> a la del Adelantado, que presenta una frente de siete casas alineadas,
> todas magníficas, desde la de doña Perfecta a la de Nicolasito
> Hernández? . . . Se figuran estos canallas que uno no ha visto
> nada, ni ha estado en París . . . (XI; 447).

Don Cayetano is one of the principal mouthpieces of this point of
view, and, as we have seen, he is concerned principally with Orbajosa's
past:

> En todas las épocas de nuestra historia, los orbajosenses se han
> distinguido por su hidalguía, por su nobleza, por su valor, por su
> entendimiento (X; 445).

Don Cayetano is also convinced, as are doña Perfecta and don
Inocencio, that Orbajosa is a virtuous city:

> Pocas localidades conocemos en que crezcan con más lozanía las
> plantas y arbustos de todas las virtudes, libres de la yerba maléfica
> de los vicios. Aquí todo es paz, mutuo respeto, humildad
> cristiana. La caridad se practica aquí como en los tiempos
> evangélicos; aquí no se conoce la envidia; aquí no se conocen las
> pasiones criminales, y si oye usted hablar de ladrones y asesinos,
> tenga por seguro que no son hijos de esta noble tierra, o que per-
> tenecen al número de los infelices pervertidos por las predicaciones
> demagógicas. Aquí verá usted el carácter nacional en toda su pureza,

recto, hidalgo, incorruptible, puro, sencillo, patriarcal, hospita-
lario, generoso (XVI; 461-462).

The virtues of Orbajosa are such that only in such cities is to be
found true religion:

Hijo mío, los habitantes de Orbajosa seremos palurdos y toscos
labriegos sin instrucción, sin finura ni buen tono; pero a lealtad y
buena fe no nos gana nadie, nadie, pero nadie (XI; 449),

affirms doña Perfecta, an ironic remark, since she has just been
commiserating with Pepe over the loss of his government commission,
a decision which she herself has engineered. The ironic nature of the
statement of don Cayetano, quoted above, is equally obvious: far
from the killing of Pepe Rey and the outbreak of civil conflict being
due to demagogues, the motive force is doña Perfecta herself, aided
and abetted by the Canon.

Orbajosa has thus a double standard of judgement, and the gap is
obvious enough between the glories of which the inhabitants boast,
and the sad state of the city in the present day. A similar gap exists
in social judgements. Far from being a city of loyalty and good faith,
Orbajosa is a hot-bed of ill-natured gossip. The *tertulias* of the Casino
are one of the centres of such gossip, and we see for example how
Pepe's alleged irreverence in the Cathedral, first reported to doña
Perfecta by various of her friends (IX; 439), gradually assumes graphic
properties, until he is credited with having entered the Cathedral
wearing a top hat and smoking. Finally, he is said to wish to pull the
Cathedral down, and build in its stead a shoe factory (XII; 453) or a
pitch works (XIV; 457). Don Inocencio early in the novel expresses
his belief that no doubt Pepe prefers the beauty of a cast-iron market-
building to those of the Cathedral (VI; 430). It is further related
that Pepe has been commissioned by English Protestants to preach
heresy throughout Spain, and that he spends all night gaming in the
Casino and staggers home drunk (XIV; 458). Galdós has presented
these details to show the way in which calumny and rumour spread,
particularly in a small town where there are few amusements other

than those derived from commenting on the faults and follies of one's acquaintances and friends.

Respectable *tertulias*, such as that at doña Perfecta's house, are insufferably dull; every night the same local dignitaries exchange the same superficial judgements and trivial opinions. The author points out that Pepe is at first able to make some friends in the Casino;

> Rey no dejó de encontrar amigos sinceros en la docta corporación, pues ni todos eran maldicientes, ni faltaban allí personas de buen sentimiento (XI; 447).

Even these he tended to alienate by his frank criticism of the town. The only *orbajosense* with whom he appears to be on good terms is don Juan Tafetán, the ex-Tenorio, now an oldish man, and a somewhat grotesque figure. But at least he has one virtue: "no era maldiciente" (XII; 451), and he befriends the unfortunate Troya sisters. These three girls are shown as being the victims of the narrow-minded prejudices of Orbajosa. Essentially they are the children of a well-to-do family which has come down in the world —a subject which Galdós was to explore further in the *novelas contemporáneas*— and they are shunned, not so much for what they are, as for what they might become. Their bad reputation arises from the fact that they are "chismosas, enredadoras, traviesas y despreocupadas" (XII; 452): that is to say, they display many of the qualities which distinguish their fellow citizens, but they make the mistake of enjoying themselves and are "condenadas por el mundo a causa de su frivolidad" (XII; 453). The tricks they get up to are not of any great significance, and indeed Galdós typifies them as "majaderías y libertades propias de los pequeños pueblos" (XII; 452). The atmosphere in which they live has formed them, and indeed preserved them from greater vices. But, having once condemned them, their fellow citizens can never bring themselves to forgive:

> Pero cualquiera que fuese la razón, ello es que el agraciado triunvirato troyano tenía sobre sí un estigma de esos que, una vez puestos por susceptible vecindario, acompañan implacablemente

hasta más allá de la tumba (XII; 452).

Balancing the Troya sisters and don Juan Tafetán we have Jacinto, another typical product of a small town, a young man who is not without intelligence but also has been formed in the old school and has acquired learning without judgement; he demonstrates a "vanidad pueril" (IX; 437), encouraged by the praise of the Canon and his doting mother. Rosario calls him "estudioso y formalito" (VIII; 434), but when we see him in the company of the Troya sisters we see how shallow he is, and how superficial is his pose of gravity and learning. Galdós himself had begun to study law in the University of Madrid, and Pepe's opinion on the dangers inherent in encouraging too many young men to study the law are no doubt the fruit of personal experience and observation. Certainly the amount of litigation in which the *orbajosenses* indulge proves the assertion of Pepe Rey that "las cuestiones se multiplican en proporción de la demanda" (VII; 433). They are, in Pepe's view —and no doubt in the eyes of Galdós— one of the causes of the political unrest in the country:

> . . . de aquí proviene ese brillante escuadrón de holgazanes, llenos de pretensiones, que fomentan la empleomanía, perturban la Política, agitan la opinión y engendran las revoluciones. De alguna parte han de comer (VII; 433).

Perhaps the greatest defect which Galdós reveals in the social customs of Orbajosa is the hostility with which the inhabitants face the outside world. The landed proprietors, small and large, are self-satisfied, smug and complacent:

> Tenían la imperturbable serenidad del mendigo, que nada apetece mientras no le falta un mendrugo para engañar el hambre y buen sol para calentarse. Lo que principalmente distinguía a los orbajosenses del Casino era un sentimiento de viva hostilidad hacia todo lo que de fuera viniese. Y siempre que algún forastero de viso se presentaba en las augustas salas, creíanle venido a poner en duda la superioridad de la patria del ajo, o a disputarle por envidia las preeminencias incontrovertibles que Natura le concediera (XI; 446).

They are fit citizens for such a desolate region. And the smaller the town, the less it has to boast about, the greater the pride of the inhabitants: "por lo mismo que son enanos suelen ser soberbios" (XI; 447). They see Madrid, as does doña Perfecta, as "aquel centro de corrupción, de envidia y rivalidades" (XI; 449). "Aquí no estamos en Madrid, señores;" says the Canon, "aquí no estamos en ese centro de corrupción, de escándalo" (XIV; 458). And don Cayetano tells Pepe:

> Aquí verá usted el carácter nacional en toda su pureza, recto, hidalgo, incorruptible, puro, sencillo, patriarcal, hospitalario, generoso . . . Por eso gusto tanto de vivir en esta pacífica soledad, lejos del laberinto de las ciudades, donde reinan, ¡ay!, la falsedad y el vicio (XVI; 462).

They firmly believe that all *madrileños* despise the provinces, and think of the inhabitants as aborigines, wearing loincloths, "y que esta ciudad es lo mismito que las de Marruecos" (XI; 447). For them it is the centre of the world, a paradise and a promised land. Their attitude is summed up by don Cayetano in one of his letters to his friend in Madrid. He sees the army as attacking, not the *facciosos*, but the traditions which Orbajosa holds most dear:

> la fe religiosa y el acrisolado españolismo, que, por fortuna, se conservan en lugares no infestados aún de la asoladora pestilencia (XXXII; 509).

Such is the opinion of a closed mind, a smug, parochial point of view which sees Orbajosa as a land of pastoral contentment and Madrid as Sodom and Gomorrah, although this is the land of the *facciosos*, of the troubles. It is little wonder that an army officer such as Pinzón can view Orbajosa as

> un pueblo dominado por gentes que enseñan la desconfianza, la superstición y el aborrecimiento a todo el género humano (XVIII; 469).

His belief is, however, coloured by his personal experiences and by the killing of his father in the vicinity of the city. Although Pepe echoes his views, at the time of the conversation, he does so only because of the rebuffs and humiliations he has suffered: his pastoral myth having been exploded, he has swung to the opposite extreme, and sees Orbajosa as a devouring monster. This is not necessarily the view of Galdós; the author believes that the inhabitants are not fundamentally wicked, but that their narrow view of life and the lack of outside standards by which to judge themselves lead to complacency, self-satisfaction, hypocrisy and false judgements. But parochialism is not a crime.

The novel does not present us with any sustained picture of Madrid society, but we must not conclude that Galdós believes that the society of the capital is much better than that of the provincial city. Pepe himself rejects the "falsedades y comedias de lo que llaman alta sociedad" (V; 427), and when he learns that Rosario cannot speak French or play the piano and does not dress elegantly —social virtues required of the young ladies of Madrid society— he exclaims:

> ¡Oh, Rosario! —exclamó con ardor el caballero—, dudaba que fueses perfecta; ahora ya sé que lo eres (VIII; 435).

And of course it is in Madrid that doña Perfecta is able to accomplish her feat of string-pulling by writing to ladies of her acquaintance. The falsities and superficialities of life in Madrid were to be one of the principal subjects of the *novelas contemporáneas* of Galdós, and hence, in these novels, the picture of the countryside changes once the emphasis is placed on the vices and corruptions of the capital. In the *novelas contemporáneas* the country becomes part of a metaphor, the other part of which is Madrid itself.

VII

The Conflict: Moral Aspects

The moral defects of small-town society have already been touched
upon. The Canon's views on the role of science in the modern world
are the result of prejudice, and he is quite prepared to believe that "el
hombre del siglo" will prefer a cast-iron market hall to a cathedral.
It is later taken for granted that Pepe has absorbed the theories of
German philosophers —a reference to the views of Krause which
were being adopted by liberal thinkers in Spain at that period— and
that he will know and agree with Darwin's theory of natural selection,
simplified grotesquely into a belief that man is descended from the
apes. Pepe is bound to be an atheist. Doña Perfecta says to him:

> Me guardaré muy bien de vituperarte porque creas que no nos crió
> Dios a su imagen y semejanza, sino que descendemos de los micos;
> ni porque niegues la existencia del alma, asegurando que ésta es
> una droga como los papelillos de magnesio o de ruibarbo que se
> venden en la botica (IX; 439).

In Madrid he must necessarily have absorbed false doctrines, and
have taken up a superficial rationalistic attitude. In thus attacking
Pepe and his supposed beliefs, the *orbajosenses* reveal their own
ignorance, but they also demonstrate an inability to listen to the
arguments of their opponents. If Pepe denies these charges, which
are to them self-evident truths, then he must be lying. They are the
only people who can be trusted to be upright, honourable and
charitable. But their actions suggest that this is far from the truth,
and that they deceive themselves.

Doña Perfecta reveals to her nephew, as we have seen, that in her
eyes the end is all-important, and that any means may be utilised to
bring about the desired goal, including lies, underhand dealing and
brute force. She has an interview with *el tío Licurgo* (X; 445), and

we later note that the entanglement of law-suits in which Pepe finds himself entrapped becomes even more complex. She is responsible for the non-arrival of the letters from Madrid, although hypocritically she upbraids *Caballuco* for failing to deliver them (XI; 448). It is her string-pulling that brings about the dismissal of Pepe, although again she lays the blame on others, on this occasion on the "politiquejos infames" (XI; 449) of Madrid. Her immoral actions are, however, fully justified in her eyes, since they are calculated to bring about a very desirable end. It is, of course, not only the *orbajosenses* who use subterfuges. The way in which Pinzón ingratiates himself with the household, and the way in which the servant is bribed and Pepe enters the house in disguise are equally reprehensible. But Pepe shows himself, in his letters to his father, truly repentant for his underhand actions. Doña Perfecta never repents, for she is sure she is in the right.

Similarly, don Inocencio, as he becomes more and more embroiled in the situation, shows an inability to distinguish between right and wrong. He allows himself to be led into preaching a holy war against the infidels of Madrid: "Yo tengo una fe ciega en el triunfo de la ley de Dios", he tells *Caballuco*:

Alguno ha de salir en defensa de ella. Si no son unos, serán otros. La palma de la victoria, y con ella la gloria eterna, alguien se la ha de llevar. Los malvados perecerán, si no hoy, mañana. Aquel que va contra la ley de Dios, caerá, no hay remedio. Sea de esta manera, sea de la otra, ello es que ha de caer. No le salvan ni sus argucias, ni sus escondites, ni sus artimañas. La mano de Dios está alzada sobre él, y le herirá su falta. Tengámosle compasión y deseemos su arrepentimiento ... En cuanto a vosotros, hijos míos, no esperéis que os diga una palabra sobre el paso que seguramente vais a dar. Sé que sois buenos; sé que vuestra determinación generosa y el noble fin que os guía lavan toda mancha pecaminosa ocasionada por el derramiento de sangre; sé que Dios os bendice; que vuestra victoria, lo mismo que vuestra muerte, os sublimarán a los ojos de los hombres y a los de Dios; sé que se os deben palmas y alabanzas y toda suerte de honores; pero, a pesar de esto, hijos míos, mi labio no os incitará a la pelea (XXII; 484).

He preaches war and hatred, but endeavours at the same time to suggest that he is a man of peace, showing the same double standards which doña Perfecta has so clearly demonstrated. And, finally, he is provoked by his niece into counselling the use of brute force. But, as we have seen, unlike doña Perfecta, he repents in the end, a man broken by his knowledge that he has transgressed against the law of his religion. As he said in the speech quoted above, "aquél que va contra la ley de Dios, caerá". He was a good man, but set in his ways and unable to distinguish between private interest and the interest of the Church. He confuses his issues, and falls into grievous sin.

The person responsible for his final fall is his niece, a woman motivated by maternal love, another example of a force in human conduct which is potentially good, but which in María Remedios is perverted by ambition. It is she who first brings up the subject of a physical attack on Pepe, no more than "un susto"; a few broken bones will soon make him change his tune, she counsels. Doña Perfecta calls her plan "una indignidad cobarde"(XXV; 490), although we may well ask if there is any difference, other than of degree, in suggesting the beating of an individual and in urging the *facciosos* to take up arms against the government. According to the standards of Orbajosa, María Remedios was a model of virtue:

> Servía cariñosamente a cuantos la necesitaban; jamás dio motivo de hablillas y murmuraciones de mal género; jamás se mezcló en intrigas. Era piadosa, no sin dejarse llevar a extremos de mojigatería chocantes; practicaba la caridad; gobernaba la casa de su tío con habilidad suprema; era bien recibida, admirada y obsequiada en todas partes . . . (XXVI; 494).

María Remedios comes from a lowly family, and always feels herself inferior to doña Perfecta, although the latter treats her with great familiarity. Her great ambition was that Jacinto should marry Rosario:

> Por esto era buena y mala; por esto era religiosa y humilde, o terrible y osada; por esto era todo cuanto hay que ser, porque, sin tal idea, María, verdadera encarnación de su proyecto, no existiría (XXVI; 494-495).

Her maternal love drives her to counsel desperate measures. The
Canon endeavours to dissuade her, saying thàt, in his belief, the
measures already taken are more appropriate and are, indeed, being
successful. He has come to the conclusion that Rosario is not the
paragon he had thought her, and that indeed Jacinto is much more
worthy than she, and he urges his niece to think no more of the possible marriage. But María Remedios is not to be moved; she is a
woman with one fixed ambition, and, like Pepe Rey, she is determined
to overcome all obstacles. She tells her uncle that he has lost his
nerve, and that it is ludicrous that doña Perfecta should think of
starting a civil war to keep Pepe and Rosario apart:

> Pero usted cree, como doña Perfecta, que va a haber una guerra y
> que para echar de aquí a don Pepe se necesita que media Nación
> se levante contra la otra media· . . . La señora se ha vuelto loca, y
> usted allá se le va (XXVI; 496-497).

The Canon counsels resignation, but she bursts into tears and imagines
what will befall her poor Jacinto. Her very appearance changes:

> Pero, de repente, transformóse el rostro de aquella mujer; mudá-
> ronse los plañideros sollozos en una voz bronca y dura; palideció
> su rostro; temblaron sus labios; cerráronse sus puños; cayéronse
> sobre la frente algunas guedejas del desordenado cabello; secáronse
> por completo sus ojos al calor de la ira que bramaba en su pecho;
> levantóse del asiento y no como una mujer, sino como una harpía,
> gritó (XXVII; 498)

that she and Jacinto must go to Madrid to seek his fortune and leave
don Inocencio for ever. The Canon is unable to withstand the wrath
of the irate mother, but still refuses to advocate "el susto". Finally,
he compromises; *Caballuco* will be asked to accompany María
Remedios because she fears that Pepe Rey will assault her — a blatant
lie. But when *Caballuco* appears, he will take his orders only from
don Inocencio, and the wretched Canon is forced by his niece to give
the order. Faced with the fury of María Remedios, we almost feel
compassion for the Canon. The driving force behind María Remedios's
outburst is thus maternal passion, an instinct for good which neverthe-

less can be extremely dangerous:

> si esta exaltación del afecto maternal no coincide con la absoluta pureza del corazón y con la honradez perfecta, suele extraviarse y convertirse en frenesí lamentable, que puede contribuir, como otra cualquiera pasión desbordada, a grandes faltas y catástrofes (XXVI; 494).

VIII

The Conflict: Political Issues

If we turn now to look at the political issues involved, we see how small-town parochialism can also become a dangerous weapon. The town itself is corrupt, and the administration is in the hands of persons who are themselves manipulated by the powerful and rich. With unconscious irony, doña Perfecta laments the resignation of the judge:

> ¡El otro era tan honrado . . . ! —dijo la señora con zozobra—. Jamás le pedí cosa alguna que al punto no me concediera (XX; 477).

This is the land of the *facción,* as we are told at the outset of the novel, and although Orbajosa had never been the scene of a great battle, its inhabitants had taken to the hills in 1827, during the first Carlist War, and again in 1848. It is the home of dynasties of *guerrilleros*: the Aceros, the *Caballucos,* the *Pelosmales.* The old *facciosos* are now found in positions of trust in the city. " ¡Qué pueblo! " comments Pinzón (XVIII; 469). And hand in hand with the fostering of rebellion goes a great distrust of the central government:

> Y con la popularidad de las partidas y de los partidarios coincidía, siempre creciente, la impopularidad de todo lo que entraba en Orbajosa con visos de Delegación o instrumento del Poder central. Los soldados fueron siempre tan mal vistos allí, que siempre que los ancianos narraban un crimen, robo, asesinato, violación o cualquier otro espantable desafuero, añadían: "Esto sucedió cuando vino la tropa" (XVIII; 468).

Pinzón fears that a new civil war is brewing up, and if this is so, then Orbajosa is sure to show signs of its coming.

> Algunos se ríen y aseguran que no puede haber otra guerra civil como la pasada. No conocen el país, no conocen a Orbajosa y sus habitantes. Yo sostengo que esto que ahora empieza lleva larga cola y que tendremos una nueva lucha cruel y sangrienta que

durará lo que Dios quiera (XVIII; 470).

We now hark back to the first chapters, and recall that Pepe had encountered violence from his first arrival in the district. Orbajosa and the *facciosos* are inseparable, and Pepe agrees that the situation is virtually insoluble:

> Pero creo que mientras esta gente no perezca y vuelva a nacer; mientras que hasta las piedras no muden de forma, no habrá paz en Orbajosa (XVIII; 469).

Pinzón is of course talking in general terms. He has come from Madrid, and it is clear from the various actions taken by Madrid —the sending of troops, the replacement of the civil authorities— that the government does feel that a dangerous situation is being brought about. But in the course of the novel we see how the national situation is exploited by the diehards of Orbajosa, and what a significant part doña Perfecta herself plays in the outcome of events. *Caballuco,* Cristóbal Ramos, has given his word to the Governor of the province that he will not take his men into the field, an assurance that must have given relief to the authorities. But for purely personal and private reasons doña Perfecta prevails upon him to break his word, whilst the Canon stands by and, if he does not openly advocate violence, tacitly approves of doña Perfecta's subtle machinations.

Caballuco is first presented to us in the opening chapters as a man of strength and determination but of limited abilities and intelligence. As we have seen, the unfortunate episode at the house of the Troya girls gives him a reason for personal animosity towards Pepe Rey, and the engineer, blinded by rage, insults him and calls him an animal. Nevertheless, *Caballuco*'s word is pledged:

> decía claramente a todo el mundo que él no quería *reñir con el Gobierno* ni *meterse en danzas* que podían costarle caras (XXI; 478).

And his word is not lightly to be broken. When he appears at doña Perfecta's house, she mocks him for having lost his manhood, for allowing soldiers to spit on him: a blatant untruth. *Caballuco* loses his temper, but refuses to break his word: "a caballero no me gana

nadie" (XXI; 479). Doña Perfecta continues to taunt him, and
finally breaks into tears at the thought of her defenceless home. It is
insinuated that Pepe Rey is at the heart of the conspiracy against
doña Perfecta, and *Caballuco* breaks out violently: " ¡Le cortaré la
cabeza al señor Rey! " (XXI; 481). Both doña Perfecta and the
Canon then tell him that they counsel no violence, and doña Perfecta
goes on to add that her real fear is that the soldiers will take Pepe's
part. *Caballuco* is told that the *facciosos* of other towns are taking to
the hills, and his local patriotism is aroused, but he still refuses to
give way:

> que si yo di mi palabra, fue porque la di, y si no salgo, es porque
> no quiero salir, y si quiero que haya partidas, las habrá, y si no
> quiero, no; porque yo soy quien soy, el mismo hombre de
> siempre, bien lo saben todos (XXI; 482).

Doña Perfecta now tries another tactic, assuring Ramos that "Eso es
muy grave, gravísimo y yo no puedo aconsejarte nada" (XXII; 482),
but she continues to make arrangements with the others present for
the gathering together of all who would be willing to rise against the
government:

> No te he aconsejado yo tal cosa, y si lo haces es por tu voluntad.
> Tampoco el señor don Inocencio te habrá dicho una palabra en
> este sentido. Pero cuando tú lo dices así, razones muy poderosas
> tendrás (XXII; 483),

she insists. Don Inocencio says that it would be improper for a
priest to counsel the use of force, and that he will not therefore say
a word, but he adds that the inhabitants of Orbajosa want the rising
to take place and that it will go down in history; nevertheless, he
insists, he will maintain a discreet silence. Doña Perfecta approves of
his position, but adds that clerics have been known to take part in
battles themselves when they have felt the fatherland and the faith
to be in danger. The Catholic faith is indeed in danger at this time,
replies don Inocencio, and the army is no more than the instrument
of the atheists and Protestants of Madrid:

Bien lo sabemos todos. En aquel centro de corrupción, de escan-
dalo, de irreligiosidad y descreimiento, unos cuantos hombres
malignos, comprados por el oro extranjero, se emplean en destruir
en nuestra España la semilla de la fe (XXII; 483-484).

A new French Revolution is at hand, and don Inocencio then begins
to preach what is in effect a holy crusade against the actual government:

Yo tengo una fe ciega en el triunfo de la ley de Dios. Alguno ha
de salir en defensa de ella. Si no son unos, serán otros. La palma
de la victoria, y con ella la gloria eterna, alguien se la ha de llevar.
Los malvados perecerán, si no hoy, mañana. Aquel que va contra
la ley de Dios, caerá, no hay remedio. Sea de esta manera, sea de
otra, ello es que ha de caer. No le salvan ni sus argucias, ni sus
escondites, ni sus artimañas. La mano de Dios está alzada sobre él,
y le herirá su falta (XXII; 484).

He continues to assert that he himself will not counsel the use of
force, and that, if necessary, he resigns himself to martyrdom.
Caballuco is carried away by the rhetoric of the priest, and feels
himself insufficient to carry into effect the great crusade, lacking as
he does cavalry and artillery, but doña Perfecta suggests that he take
the latter from the enemy and assures him that his heart is great.
Caballuco is finally won over, and shouts: " ¡Viva Orbajosa!   ¡Muera
Madrid!" (XXII; 485).

It is evident how doña Perfecta works on *Caballuco*'s personal
pride, on his local patriotism and on his religious faith. *Caballuco* is
a man of honour —"yo soy quien soy", he says, echoing the words
of many a hero of a Golden Age play— and his word has been given.
But he is like putty in the hands of the astute doña Perfecta, and it is
noteworthy that it is don Inocencio's appeal to religion that at the
last wins him over. In the confrontation between doña Perfecta and
Caballuco, don Inocencio literally keeps his promise by not in actual
words inciting *Caballuco* to violent action, but his religious fervour
has the desired effect. It is in the scene with María Remedios and the
Canon, to which I have already alluded, that *Caballuco* is finally
ordered to use force by don Inocencio. Both doña Perfecta and the

Canon are now implicated, and the faction has been sent out into the field against its declared intention, and in violation of the agreement with the Governor of the province.

The appearance of the *facciosos* of Orbajosa in the field is therefore strictly linked to the plot of the novel, and it is made clear that doña Perfecta and don Inocencio have an evident responsibility for what is likely to occur. In an effort to ensure that Pepe Rey is finally driven from the town, doña Perfecta equates her nephew with the government of Madrid:

> Mi sobrino, por una serie de fatalidades, que son otras tantas pruebas de los males pasajeros que a veces permite Dios para nuestro castigo, equivale a un ejército, equivale a la autoridad del Gobierno, equivale al alcalde, equivale al juez; mi sobrino no es mi sobrino: es la nación oficial, Remedios; es esa segunda nación, compuesta de los perdidos que gobiernan en Madrid, y que se ha hecho dueña de la fuerza material; de esa nación aparente, porque la real es la que calla, paga y sufre; de esa nación ficticia que firma al pie de los decretos, y pronuncia discursos, y hace una farsa de gobierno, y una farsa de autoridad, y una farsa de todo. Eso es hoy mi sobrino; es preciso que te acostumbres a ver lo interno de las cosas. Mi sobrino es el Gobierno, el Brigadier, el alcalde nuevo, el juez nuevo, porque todos le favorecen a causa de la unanimidad de sus ideas; porque son uña y carne, lobos de la misma manada . . . Entiéndelo bien: hay que defenderse de todos ellos, porque todos son uno, y uno es todos; hay que atacarlos en conjunto, y no con palizas al volver de una esquina, sino como atacaban nuestros abuelos a los moros, a los moros, Remedios (XXV; 491).

The reference to the Moors is clearly of the utmost significance. The insurrection is presented as a holy war in defence of the faith, and the opposing factions view each other with a bitterness which suggests that the war will be bloody and cruel; "Es cuestión de moros y cristianos" (XXV; 491). Pepe Rey himself, in one of his letters to his father, recognises the course which events are taking:

> La hostilidad contra nosotros y contra el Gobierno la tienen los orbajosenses en su espíritu, formando parte de él como la fe religiosa (XXVIII; 502).

There can be no turning back. But we must remember that, in terms of the novel, the war is the result of family tensions, the result of doña Perfecta's blind belief that her way of life is the only true one, and that her nephew represents not only a different way of life but the road to moral perdition. She is quite clearly sincere in this mistaken belief. Galdós does not want us to doubt her sincerity, but seeks to show how personal animosities can embitter an already difficult political situation, and how civil factions grow out of petty causes which are in their turn based on blindness, mistrust and an egoistic belief in the sacredness of one's cause and the rightness of one's judgments. By a final irony, as we see through don Cayetano's letters at the end of the novel, the civil war breaks out after the death of Pepe, after, that is to say, the cause of the original friction has been removed. Don Cayetano, writing from the peace of his library, and blinded by self-interest, can say, and sincerely believe, that:

> Yo deploro esta guerra, que va tomando proporciones alarmantes; pero reconozco que nuestros bravos campesinos no son responsables de ella, pues han sido provocados al cruento batallar por la audacia del Gobierno, por la desmoralización de sus sacrílegos delegados, por la saña sistemática con que los representantes del Estado atacan lo más venerado que existe en la conciencia de los pueblos: la fe religiosa y el acrisolado españolismo, que, por fortuna, se conservan en lugares no infestados aún de la asoladora pestilencia (XXXII; 509).

We, the readers, are only too aware that the inciting of the *facciosos* of Orbajosa is the work of doña Perfecta, with the tacit assistance of don Inocencio.

We may now turn to consider the question of the symbolism of the characters. How far do they stand for political attitudes? Some striking symbolism is applied to the relationship between Pepe Rey and Rosario. Pepe complains that the troubles he has met in Orbajosa are crucifying him, and Galdós speaks also in terms of his martyrdom:

> Entregó su cuerpo y su alma a los sayones, que esgrimieron horribles hojas de papel sellado, mientras la víctima, elevando los ojos al Cielo, decía para sí con cristiana mansedumbre: "Padre mío, ¿por qué me has abandonado? " (XI; 450).

The obvious comparisons with Christ[7] —which no doubt shocked many nineteenth-century readers— are further accentuated in the scene in the chapel, where Rosario suffers a transformation which suggests the resurrection of Lazarus: "Haré lo que me dices: me levanto y te sigo" (XVII; 465). She sees light streaming from Pepe, and their meeting ends with the cockcrow. Looking back to the political symbolism of *La Fontana de Oro*, it is easy to see a comparison between Rosario and Clara, and between Pepe Rey and the significantly named Lázaro. Rosario —brought up in a life of religious observances in a restricted, narrow world— can be taken to represent the spirit of Spain, torn between Pepe Rey (the hope for the future) and doña Perfecta (the appeal to the past). No doubt this obvious symbolism was in Galdós's mind. But if we try to relate the action of the novel to the political events of his day, the relationship becomes less clear. It takes place after 1870 (the year of Pepe's journey abroad) and a few years before 1876 (the date of publication):

> Como dato de no escaso interés, apuntaremos que lo que aquí se va contando ocurrió en un año que no está muy cerca del presente, ni tampoco muy lejos . . . (XVIII; 468).

We must therefore imagine the action taking place about 1872.[8]

In 1868 Isabel II had been removed from the throne, and an attempt had been made, not for the first time, to create a truly constitutional monarchy in Spain. In October 1870 the Crown was accepted by Amadeo of Savoy, but already the coalition which had brought about the Revolution was in disarray. Amadeo's reign was brief, and on 11 February 1873 he abdicated. The Republicans attempted to create a Federal Republic, but this too failed to command authority, and was overthrown in its turn by a military uprising on

[7]Compare the article of J. Lowe, 10.

[8]Dr N. G. Round has pointed out to me that María Remedios makes a reference in passing to the Paris *commune* of 1871: "Algo de esa gente que quemó a París con petróleo" (XXV; 491).

2 January 1874. A further military revolt in December of the same year brought to the throne Alfonso XII, the son of Isabel. The First Republic had been destroyed by party rivalry, by the dogmatic anti-clericalism of the Republicans, by the revolt of the Cantonalist extremists and by the outbreak in 1873 of the Second Carlist War. By 1874 the Carlist cause reached the height of its success, and in the north of Spain a separate Carlist state was created. One of the decisive features of this turbulent period was the demonstration that, in the words of Raymond Carr, "the existence of any régime in Spain was a function of the loyalty of the army" (13, 342). None of the governments which attempted to hold power after the Revolution of 1868 could provide either order or stability, and the Restoration succeeded because it promised a more stable political structure than its predecessors.

It was against this background that Galdós wrote his novel. In his journalistic writings, in *La Nación* (1865-1868), in *La Revista de España* (1871-1872) and in *La Ilustración* (1872), Galdós comments on the political happenings of the day. Condemning war as a barbarous solution of national differences, he preaches the spirit of conciliation. Rejecting the extremes of Federalism and Carlism, he demonstrates that, despite the differences of their political ideologies, both forces are working towards the destruction of civilised values:

> Aunque con distinto ideal, el carlismo y la demagogia comunista tienen muchos puntos de contacto, sobre todo en los procedimientos por uno y otro empleados para conseguir su fin, y como enemigos ambos de la sociedad moderna cuyos principios atacan sañudamente desde opuesto lado.[9]

Nigel Glendinning has pointed out that similar views are to be found in *La Fontana de Oro*:

> In *La Fontana de Oro* the situations of the 1820s which arose as

[9]Benito Pérez Galdós, *Crónica de la quincena,* ed., with a preliminary study, by W. H. Shoemaker (Princeton, 1948), 100.

a result of extremist and intolerant views in religion and politics, are relevant also to the revolutionary period of 1868 (17, 42).

The same critic has pointed out the political relevance of the first series of the *Episodios nacionales* for Galdós's contemporaries:

> Ultimately the reasons for divisions in Spanish society are not simply political, but also the greed, envy, ambition and violence of many individual members (17, 57).

It is in this way that we should seek a reflection in *Doña Perfecta* of the political events of the years immediately preceding its publication. We must not expect to find a close correlation between historical events and the somewhat melodramatic plot of the novel: Galdós does not wish us to infer that doña Perfecta was responsible for the outbreak of the Second Carlist War, or for the violence of Federal and Cantonalist reactions to the central government. It is tempting to assume that there are some detailed reflections of the period. The law-suits in which Pepe Rey is involved in Orbajosa may be reminiscent of the practice in the provinces during the First Republic of abolishing absentee landlordism, and in particular of the backstairs negotiations which characterised such practices. But it would be wrong to insist too much on such detailed historical parallels. Galdós was trying to set forth the basic causes for the civil strife which characterised the Spain of his day, and these he found to be rooted in the ambition, the greed and the violence of individuals, the lack of concern for political unity and the disinclination to appeal to reason, tolerance and understanding. In 1872 Galdós appealed for "un antagonismo lógico y fecundo, en vez de esta guerra torpe y salvaje" (*Revista de España*, XXV, 140).

> The faith of Galdós and other liberals in common sense and an instinct for good government, which they believed to exist particularly among city dwellers, was perhaps naive, and yet their constant criticism of those who contributed to the political instability of Spain cannot be said to reflect a lack of political purpose or justification (17, 59).

In 1872 Galdós further wrote:

Cuando los hombres se agrupan por resentimientos, cuando antiguos rencores, o la fuerza de palabras consagradas, les sirve de enlace, las colectividades . . . sólo sirven para despertar en los hombres innobles ambiciones, para avivar la repugnante envidia, para producir inmorales elevaciones y desastrosas caídas, para someter lo más caro y lo más sagrado que hay en el mundo, que es la suerte de la nación, a la tremenda prueba de una constante y abominable intriga, único ejercicio de los espíritus turbados y cegados por la pasión (*Revista de España*, XXIV, 149).

Orbajosa is clearly a symbol. Chapter II is headed "Un viaje por el corazón de España", and later in the novel the author insists that it is useless to seek the prototype of this city in any particular town or city, situated at some distance from a railway, 172 kilometres from Madrid:

Orbajosa . . . no está muy lejos ni tampoco muy cerca de Madrid, no debiendo tampoco asegurarse que enclave sus gloriosos cimientos al Norte ni al Sur, ni al Este ni al Oeste, sino que es posible esté en todas partes, y por doquiera que los españoles revuelvan sus ojos y sientan el picar de sus ajos (XVIII; 468).

Orbajosa is a symbol of attitudes. Whatever the exact correlation with the circumstances leading to the outbreak of the Second Carlist War, Galdós is endeavouring in this novel to trace its root causes, and these he finds in blind local patriotism rooted in a lack of knowledge, and the fanatical defence of a mythical Spain against the encroachment of a new order of things which is also utterly falsified in the minds of its opponents. But, before we conclude that Galdós is entirely on the side of Madrid, and completely opposed to Orbajosa, we must remember that it takes two sides to fight a civil war. Below the surface dissensions we discover Galdós's viewpoint that man has a capacity for good, but that this capacity can be twisted and perverted with dangerous ease. We are all savages under the skin. Given a less restricted background, a man like *Caballuco* could turn his energies to the good of his country; he is a man full of vitality and not without a sense of personal integrity. But his narrow upbringing has made him only too liable to fall victim to the pressures and moral blackmail of others. Pepe Rey is a man who is, in the eyes of Galdós, undertaking tasks which are to the future benefit of Spain, but, under situations of stress, the most modern "hombre del siglo" can fall back into barbarism. Until good faith can be established, and hatred and ignorance banished, society is in constant peril of being divided at any point in time, and perhaps for the most trivial of reasons, into "moros y cristianos".

In the first version of the novel, published in the *Revista de España*, Galdós can be seen as putting the blame much more squarely on the inhabitants of Orbajosa. The significant differences are in the final chapters, in the letters written by don Cayetano. There the pedant reveals how, once Pepe Rey was dead and Rosario locked in an asylum, the aspirations of María Remedios came at last to a some-what improbable fruition, in the arrangement of a marriage between doña Perfecta and the young lawyer, Jacinto. Don Cayetano tells his friend that "Perfecta se conserva muy bien y ahora ha echado carnes y se ha puesto muy guapa", an unlikely reaction to the madness of a loved daughter. Don Cayetano goes on to say that there is a difference of twenty-two years between the couple, and that he doubts that "tal unión sea provechosa". In his final letter he states that the marriage was about to take place, but that during the wedding preparations Jacinto was killed accidentally, slipping on a piece of offal and being impaled on a knife held by his mother. In this version Galdós is clearly endeavouring to suggest an ending which produces an effect of poetic justice: the machinations of María Remedios bring about the death of her adored son. But this melodramatic ending is exceptionally crude and the effect it produces is laughable. This version is the novel of a Very Angry Young Man. In the later version, the one now generally available and read, the final vision of doña Perfecta given up to religious observances, of a dead religion preying on the dead, is much more effective. Galdós recognised in the later version that his artistic judgment was seriously at fault in his first ending, and that he had allowed the needs of his polemic to twist his aesthetic judgment.

IX

Stylistic Features

The novel has many interesting stylistic features. There is much
that is Romantic about *Doña Perfecta*. The lovers feel themselves to
be predestined for each other, and love is seen as a bond which should
override other considerations. Pepe Rey writes to his father that
doña Perfecta sees the situation in medieval terms:

> la pobre señora, que tiene el feudalismo en la médula de los huesos,
> ha imaginado que voy a atacar su casa para robarle a su hija, como
> los señores de la Edad Media embestían un castillo enemigo para
> consumar cualquier desafuero (XXVIII; 502).

Indeed, his vision of Orbajosa as a ferocious beast suggests that Pepe
can be considered as a paladin attempting to rescue the damsel from
the claws of the monster. This is of course an oversimplification,
since Pepe's shining armour is tarnished through succumbing to the
temptation to use underhand and devious methods. But much of the
atmosphere of the Romantic novel persists in the story. The
conscience-stricken Rosario feels Becquerian serpents gnawing at her
heart: "Dentro de mí, una gran culebra me muerde y me envenena el
corazón" (XXIV; 487).

The use of opposed images of light and darkness is also evident and
suggests the Romantic use of contrasts, and of the pathetic fallacy.
Don Inocencio first appears as "una larga opacidad negra" (V; 427),
the light glinting on his spectacles. After the mutual declaration of
love in the garden, "una dulce sombra se extendía por la parte baja de
la huerta, mientras el último rayo del sol poniente coronaba de
resplandores las cimas de los árboles" (VIII; 436). But soon the
imagery of darkness is to be far from gentle. When doña Perfecta
tells Pepe that she will influence Rosario to forgive him for his attack
on the vestments of the images in the cathedral, Pepe feels that "por
su pensamiento pasaba una nube" (X; 444). Just before he meets the

Troya girls, Pepe gambles in the Casino, but this cannot relieve "el sombrío estado de su alma" (XII; 451). As night falls, Pepe looks out of his window, contemplating "la negrura de la noche":

> La sombra no le permitía ver las flores de la tierra ni las del cielo, que son las estrellas. La misma falta casi absoluta de claridad producía el efecto de un ilusorio movimiento en las masas de árboles que se extendían al parecer; iban perezosamente y regresaban enroscándose, como el oleaje de un mar de sombras. Formidable flujo y reflujo, una lucha entre fuerzas no bien manifiestas, agitaban la silenciosa esfera. Contemplando aquella extraña proyección de su alma sobre la noche, el matemático decía:
> —La batalla será tremenda. Veremos quién sale triunfante (XVI; 462).

The darkness of the night is thus a projection of his own misgivings, in true Romantic fashion. There then follows the scene in the chapel, in Chapter XVII which is entitled "Luz a obscuras". Apparently the situation is clarifying. Pepe has been able to see Rosario, and knows now that she loves him. As day dawns, the soldiers ride into the town, and the first reaction is that new life is being introduced into the silent, dying city:

> La ciudad era tristeza, silencio, vejez; el Ejército, alegría, estrépito, juventud. Entrando el uno en la otra, parecía que la momia recibía por arte maravilloso el don de la vida, y bulliciosa saltaba fuera del húmedo sarcófago para bailar en torno de él. ¡Qué movimiento, qué algazara, qué risa, qué jovialidad! No existe nada tan interesante como un ejército. Es la Patria en su aspecto juvenil y vigoroso (XVIII; 467).

A new hope is born. However, Galdós follows the description of the army with an account of the reception of troops in small cities, the fears they evoke, the reprisals they take and engender. And, as the plot unfolds, we can see that the lightening of this chapter has indeed been momentary; the gloom increases, and Pepe is shot in the darkness of the garden. The final description of doña Perfecta adds to the gloom:

> Ahora parece que hay una nube negra encima de nosotros. La pobre Perfecta habla frecuentemente de esta nube, que cada vez

se pone más negra, mientras ella se vuelve cada día más amarilla (XXXII; 511).

The garden of doña Perfecta's house is linked throughout the novel with the love of Rosario and Pepe. Their first conversation is near the window overlooking the garden, and they are sent by doña Perfecta to walk there. This scene is not described, but on the following day comes the declaration of love which takes place, as we have seen, in the same spot. Rosario, after she is imprisoned, steals out to the garden to see Pepe, but by that time the dominant image in the novel is that of darkness, and it is in the darkness of the *huerta,* where Pepe has gone to meet Rosario again and take her from her mother's grasp, that the engineer meets his death. We recall that when the garden is first mentioned, as Pepe Rey rides for the first time towards his aunt's house, *el tío Licurgo* says that it formerly had a door or gate, "pero la señora la mandó tapiar" (II; 421). The potential Garden of Eden becomes a dark cell, a graveyard.

Similar symbolic use is made of sound patterns in the novel. The train whistle at the opening of the novel awakens the sleeping country-side, a symbol of the hope for the future which is later echoed by the cockcrow, so closely followed by the bugles of the troops. The typical sounds of Orbajosa are those of hooves striking the cobbles of the streets, and the creaking weathercock of the Cathedral. And in the countryside the typical sound is that of the shot. The smoke of the train finds a sinister parallel in the smoke from the barrels of the guns of the Civil Guard, and these shots are echoed at the end of the novel in the two shots fired in the garden, which result in the death of Pepe. The gaily twittering birds of the garden, described when Pepe first arrives at the house, give way to the chirping of insects:

Aquí, un chirrido áspero; allí, un chasquido semejante al que hacemos con la lengua; allá, lastimeros murmullos; más lejos, un son vibrante parecido al de la esquila suspendida al cuello de la res vagabunda (XVI; 462), in which it is not hard to find a parallel to the many problems which beset and irritate Pepe Rey at this point in the action. Too much should not be read into this simple use of sounds, but it is typical of the later Galdós that realistic description is used to convey at the same time symbolic overtones which are an aid to the understanding of the novel and add depth and significance to the descriptions.

Animal imagery is also well employed. The nickname *Caballuco* suggests a centaur, a being who is a combination of man and beast. Pepe calls him "un animal" (as does María Remedios: XXX; 504), but, as we have seen, he also shows, after his own fashion, a strong sense of honour. As the final tragic situation develops, María Remedios rushes to doña Perfecta's house to warn her of Pepe's plans. Doña Perfecta reacts "con una especie de bramido". The two women rush downstairs into the garden, "como dos culebras". Doña Perfecta peers into the night: "Exploró doña Perfecta la obscuridad con sus ojos llenos de ira. El rencor les daba la singular videncia de la raza felina" (XXXI; 507). These images clearly serve to suggest the bestialising effect of such emotions as jealousy and rage.

Similar patent use is made in the novels of significant names, a practice which, as Hans Hinterhäuser has pointed out (**15**, 284-285), occurs frequently not only in the novels of Galdós, but in many periods of time and in the literatures of many countries. Some names are ironic: doña Perfecta, don Inocencio. Some describe a principal characteristic of the personage: Rosario has been brought up in the strict practice of her religion; *el tío Licurgo,* his name recalling that of the classical law-giver, Lycurgus, is much given to law-suits; and, of course, *Caballuco.* Some names are both ironic and suggestive at the same time, the best example in this novel being the combination of the Canon's Christian and surnames: don Inocencio Tinieblas.

An interesting parallel can be drawn between the novelist's technique and that of a typical home entertainment of the late eighteenth and nineteenth centuries, the magic lantern. When Galdós begins a chapter: "Poco después había cambiado la escena" (VIII; 433), or more significantly, "La escena cambia. Ved una estancia hermosa, clara, humilde, alegre, cómoda y de un aseo sorprendente" (XXV; 489), we are reminded of the magic-lantern lecture. This same device is to be found in many nineteenth-century novelists, including Dickens and, in Spain, Pardo Bazán.

A similar technique is also employed in a dream sequence. In his later novels Galdós shows a keen interest in unusual mental states, in the behaviour of the human mind when rational control is loosened, or lost. After her confession to God, Rosario falls into an uneasy sleep, and re-creates in her dreams the events of the past few hours. She dreams that she had gone downstairs and that she sees through the glass door of the dining-room the figures of doña Perfecta, don Inocencio, *el tío Licurgo* and *Caballuco*. The description is worth quoting in full:

A la luz de la lámpara del comedor veía de espaldas a su madre. El penitenciario estaba a la derecha, y su perfil se descomponía de un modo extraño; crecíale la nariz, asemejábase al pico de un ave inverosímil, y toda su figura se tornaba en una recortada sombra, negra y espesa, con ángulos aquí y allí, irrisoria, escueta y delgada. Enfrente estaba *Caballuco,* más semejante a un dragón que a un hombre. Rosario veía sus ojos verdes, como dos grandes linternas de convexos cristales. Aquel fulgor y la imponente figura del animal le infundían miedo. *El tío Licurgo* y los otros tres se le presentaban como figuritas grotescas. Ella había visto, en alguna parte, sin duda en los muñecos de barro de las ferias, aquel reír estúpido, aquellos semblantes toscos y aquel mirar lelo. El dragón agitaba sus brazos, que, en vez de accionar, daban vueltas como aspas de molino, y revolvía de un lado para otro los globos verdes, tan semejantes a los fanales de una farmacia. Su mirar cegaba . . . La conversación parecía interesante. El penitenciario agitaba las alas. Era una presumida avecilla que quería volar y no podía. Su pico se alargaba y se retorcía. Erizábansele las plumas con síntomas de furor, y después, recogiéndose y aplacándose, escondía la pelada cabeza bajo el ala. Luego, las figurillas de barro se agitaban, queriendo ser personas, y Frasquito González se empeñaba en pasar por hombre (XXIV; 488).

Rosario is here re-creating in a dream the scene already described in which *Caballuco* is persuaded to go back on his word to the Governor. Under considerable emotional stress, her subconscious mind reveals the "true" significance of the scene which has just taken place, and the "true" characteristics of the participants. The Canon becomes a bird of prey, a dark shadow, *Caballuco* a fiery dragon, and the emphasis, placed largely on these two figures, serves to suggest even more definitely the guilt of don Inocencio for what is to come. The distortion is due in part to an optical effect, and the shadow puppets — for such they are despite the unrealistic stress on eyes— are acting out a black comedy which will have truly tragic implications. The symbolism continues, as Rosario dreams that she moved away, and saw a figure in blue military uniform at the window of Pinzon's room: "brillaban en su cuerpo los botones como sarta de lucecillas" (XXIV; 488). We already know that Pepe had bribed the servant with the intention of entering the house disguised as Pinzón, and this stratagem is hinted at in Rosario's dream. The bright shining buttons suggest a moment of hope, a gleam of light in the darkness, but as she approaches, strong arms snatch at her and bear her away. This puppet-like dream sequence epitomises the brutal actions which doña Perfecta and don Inocencio have set in train. And, as she is borne away, Rosario hears the thunderclap of sound which signifies the splitting of the table by *Caballuco*'s fist — a split which is symbolic of the civil war to come, and another sound effect which is literally a *coup de théâtre*.

The whole of this sequence, then, is cast in the form of a dream, and thus the actions of doña Perfecta and her associates are doubly deformed. As Vicente Gaos has said:

La misma escena que, dos capítulos antes, Galdós había tratado con técnica realista, es sometida ahora a una corrección enérgica de perspectiva. Ahora la contemplamos, no nosotros mismos, sino por medio de un personaje, quien, a su vez, la divisa a través de una doble rectificación visual. Es la imagen de una imagen.[10]

[10]Vicente Gaos, "Notas sobre la técnica de Galdós", *Insula*, VII, no 82,

The scene not only throws a new light on the episode in which
Caballuco had been persuaded to break his word, but it also reveals
the reaction of Rosario to the events, the emotional stress under
which she is labouring being sufficiently strong to break the habitual
restraints imposed by custom and upbringing.[11] This technique was
later to be much developed in novels such as *Angel Guerra.*

The structure of the novel has been studied by Sherman Eoff. He
believes that there are three decisive developments in the plot: Pepe
Rey's "vehement defence of science at the end of Chapter VIII";
Pepe's announcement that he is determined to marry Rosario; and
Doña Perfecta's order for the killing of her nephew. The critic
argues:

> That the three decisive steps which mark the course of an
> intensifying passion of hate together constitute one major episode,
> or plateau, in character development, becomes clear from a
> comparison of doña Perfecta's personality before and after the
> dramatic set of circumstances which provides the severe test of
> character.

He also points to the importance of the statement that doña Perfecta's
husband had been a reckless gambler and a womaniser, suggesting
that this "affords a plausible explanation for doña Perfecta's self-
sufficiency and her recourse to formalistic religious activity as
compensation for an unhappy married life". The author's aim,
according to Eoff, is

> to show how a person will continue along a challenged line of
> conduct as if to prove its justification by stubborn persistence
> (7, 65-66).

This view of the novel does not take into account doña Perfecta's
attitude to her nephew on his arrival in Orbajosa, nor does it

October 1952, 5. See also Joseph Schraibman, **12,** 59-63.

[11]Cf., in *La Fontana de Oro,* the vision of the Porreño sisters as evil birds of
prey which Clara experiences when in a state of emotion brought about by
fatigue and terror.

adequately describe Pepe Rey's role in the outcome of events. Clearly there is a gradual build-up to the violent climax of the novel, but a close reading of the early chapters shows, as I have argued, that the reader is also being prepared from the start for this dénouement through the use of stylistic devices and irony.

Stephen Gilman has suggested that the structure of the novel recalls that of the neo-classical tragedy:

> El curso entero y la estructura del libro posee, pues, los rasgos del modelo clásico: la perfección sucumbe a la imperfección en una serie de extensos actos teatrales. En pocas palabras podemos dividirlos así: 1º, introducción y primer encuentro (capítulos 1 a 17); 2º, tensión creciente, maniobras y contramaniobras (capítulos 8 a 12); 3º, intervención de factores externos, como las niñas de Troya y la situación política, que vienen a agudizar el conflicto (capítulos 13 a 18); 4º, Pepe descubre el alcance y sentido de su oposición, el necesario descubrimiento trágico (capítulo 19); 5º, su lucha final y la muerte (capítulos 20 a 31); 6º, epílogo (capítulos 32 y 33).[12]

This is a more detailed and satisfying analysis than that of Eoff. Whilst it may be going too far to suggest that the similarity between the structure of the novel and that of a neo-classical tragedy is deliberate, the form of the novel does show a dramatic development, which made it eminently suitable for theatrical adaptation. The clash of opposing forces is far more evident here than in the later novels, which aim rather at synthesis and reconciliation.

It is pertinent to inquire how far the publication of the novel in its first version in instalments influenced its form. Novels intended for publication in serial form tend to produce a rhythmical series of crises at approximately equal intervals, owing to the need to leave the reader impatient for the sequel. Whilst Galdós does not appear to have written his novel with this in mind, we have already seen that the need to write to a fixed time schedule may have been

[12]*Nueva Revista de Filología Hispánica,* III (1949), 358-359.

responsible for the unsatisfactory ending of the novel in its first version. The author himself wrote to his friend and fellow-novelist, *Clarín* (Leopoldo Alas):

> . . . la comencé sin saber cómo había de desarrollar el asunto. La escribí a empujones, quiero decir, a trozos, como iba saliendo, pero sin dificultad, con cierta afluencia que ahora no tengo.[13]

José F. Montesinos quotes this letter and concludes that the ending of the first version of *Doña Perfecta* "sólo puede ser resultado de una aberración producida por la prisa o por la fatiga" (4, I, 178). The second version, as we have seen, has an ending much more in consonance with the rest of the novel.

Doña Perfecta, then, shows signs of evident haste and was written, according to the author's own confession, "a vuelo de pluma", almost as a Romantic writer might have dashed off a narrative poem or an exuberant lyric. It has the defects, particularly in the first version, which arise from such haste. But in the second version, a tense dramatic struggle develops which, after a strong climax, is resolved into a sombre, but fitting, dénouement. However, the novel is more than a neo-classical tragedy in the form of a nineteenth-century novel, with a hero who suffers from a moral defect and who undergoes a sudden reversal of fortune. By means of imagery and symbolism, and by the skilful use of irony, Galdós prepares his readers for the final outcome. If he was not yet the complete master of his chosen instrument, he was quickly learning how to handle it to the greatest effect.

[13]Letter to *Clarín* quoted in Leopoldo Alas, *Galdós* (Madrid, 1912), 27.

X

Conclusion

The novel is, thus, the work of a young artist still unsure of his powers. His first version proved unsatisfactory, and the ending is considerably modified in the second version. *Doña Perfecta* displays many of the stylistic devices and thematic interests which Galdós was later to develop and refine: the symbolism of light and darkness, the use of natural settings, the pointed detail in the descriptions, sounds and visual effects, the interest in unusual mental states. But the primary intention is polemical. The novel is clearly intended to serve as a warning for the day in which it was written. Harking back to the issues which had underlain the power struggle in the period after the Revolution of 1868, Galdós endeavours to isolate root causes. He points to the narrow conservative views of small communities, their obscurantism and prejudice. But he does not champion the cause of Madrid. In his *novelas contemporáneas* Madrid is described as a shallow and frivolous society, and these are the defects which Pepe Rey himself sees in the society of the capital. The novel should not be read as being entirely on the side of centralised government, and against the *patria chica*.

At the end of the novel Galdós states that his purpose has been to depict "las personas que parecen buenas y no lo son" (XXXIII; 511). This has often been taken to refer specifically to doña Perfecta and to don Inocencio. But is this how the novelist intended us to react? What are the true causes of the events depicted in the novel? I have suggested earlier that the characters tend to view the world through the distorting lenses of their particular prejudices, and this is as true of the "good" characters as it is of the "bad". Whilst don Inocencio constructs his own mythical view of an Arcadian Orbajosa, and whilst doña Perfecta sees the city as an epitome of all the *castizo* virtues of old Spain, Pepe too has created for himself at the outset of the novel a prejudiced and favourable view of Orbajosa, a view which later turns to an equally prejudiced black-and-white view of the falsity of the values of this society. Doña Perfecta's narrow view of religion overcomes her first genuinely loving reaction to Pepe, and distorts her view of him. But Rosario's view of Pepe is equally distorted, for she is consumed by love for him. The clash of prejudices becomes a clash of personalities as the novel develops, and the lesson is clear: we must look reality in the face, and not allow our judgments to be warped by emotions, particularly the base emotions of jealousy, envy, anger and spite. If we do not do this, if our reason is always clouded by our emotions, then the rifts which inevitably occur in human societies will widen and the differences between classes, between creeds and view-points will acquire gigantic proportions so that in the end no concessions will be possible: all will end in struggle, in the waste of human potentialities for good, in an over-simplified polarisation of Them and Us, of "moros y cristianos". The lesson of the novel, although applicable to the political situation of the Spain of the 1870s, is basically a moral lesson.

The values which the novel supports are not so strictly defined as the weaknesses and vices which it condemns. Nevertheless, the potential for good is to be seen in the love of Pepe Rey and Rosario, a love which unites and which shows a promise for the future. In their love, Pepe and Rosario transcend the narrow religion of Orbajosa: the lovers incarnate the essence of religion, a religion of Love which has undeniably Romantic antecedents and which was to be the theme of Galdós's next major novel, *Gloria.* Love and honesty, clearness of vision and charity, these are the virtues on which Galdós's hope for the future is built. The new Spain will emerge once the age-old myths are seen to be false, and the prejudices of the past are safely buried. The achievement of this aim depends upon sane education, which alone can banish ignorance, and on clear-eyed self-knowledge, humility and charity.

But the novel itself ends in disaster, and it is evident that the novelist intended it to serve as a warning to his contemporaries, and as an indication of the path which he feared that Spain might be taking, a path which would lead inevitably to further differences and dissensions, and to the preservation of deep-rooted prejudices and rancours, bearing within them the seeds of inevitable civil strife. In his later years he appears to have come to the gloomy conclusion that no change for the better had taken place. In a letter dated 18 April 1908, he stated that "la intolerancia y bigotismo de este país . . . han cambiado poco desde 1896, fecha de *Doña Perfecta*".[14] Twelve years earlier, in 1896, acknowledging a painting of Orbajosa by the artist Aureliano de Beruete, Galdós had written:

> Veinte años ha que fue sacado de las tinieblas este castizo y turbulente poblachón y muy lejos de extinguirse su fama y de oscurecerse su historia, han crecido una y otra a tal punto que ya no hay en España provinciano capital que no sea más o menos Orbajoroído. Orbajosa encontrará Vd. en las aldeas, Orbajosa en las ciudades ricas y populosas. Orbajosa revive en las cabañas y en los dorados palacios. Todo es y todo será mañana Orbajosa, si Dios no se apiada de nosotros . . . que no se apiadará.[15]

And at the foot of the letter, he gives his address as "Madrijosa".[16]

[14]Letter to Miss Ada M. Coe, printed in the *Hispanic Review,* XIV (1946), 340-342. The date 1896 indicates that Galdós was referring to the dramatised version of the novel.

[15]Robert J. Weber, "Galdós and Orbajosa", *Hispanic Review,* XXXI (1963), 348-349.

[16]I am indebted to Professor Arthur Terry and Dr N. G. Round for helpful comments on this study.

Bibliographical Note

Editions

There is no edition of *Doña Perfecta* which can be recommended with complete confidence. The edition here used is that of F. C. Sainz de Robles. Benito Pérez Galdós, *Obras completas,* 7th ed. (Madrid, Aguilar, 1969), Vol. IV, pp. 415-511.

Biography

1. Berkowitz, H. Chonon. *Pérez Galdós, Spanish Liberal Crusader,* Madison, Wis., 1948. The fullest biography of the novelist.

General Studies

2. Casalduero, Joaquín. *Vida y obra de Galdós.* Madrid, 1951. The life of the novelist and his writing, briefly considered. Casalduero's insights are illuminating, but he tends to overstress a rigid pattern which he sees in the novelist's development.
3. Gullón, Ricardo. *Galdós, novelista moderno.* Madrid, 1960. A slighter study of the novelist and his writings.
4. Montesinos, José F. *Galdós.* Madrid, 1968-, 3 vols. The fullest critical survey of the novelist's work. Intended as an introduction to Galdós, it does not take full account of recent critical investigations.

Critical Studies

5. Varey, J. E. "Galdós in the Light of Recent Criticism", in *Galdós Studies,* ed. J. E. Varey (London, 1970), 1-35. A survey of criticism since 1943.
6. Correa, Gustavo. *El simbolismo religioso en las novelas de Pérez*

Galdós. Madrid, 1962. Chapter II is a study of the religious symbolism in *Doña Perfecta,* which suffers from being taken in isolation.

7. Eoff, Sherman. *The Novels of Pérez Galdós. The Concept of Life as Dynamic Process.* Saint Louis, 1954. An interesting but tendentious study of the structure of the novels.

8. Gilman, Stephen. "Las referencias clásicas de *Doña Perfecta*: tema y estructura de la novela", *Nueva Revista de Filología Hispánica,* III (1949), 353-362. One of the few detailed studies of a stylistic aspect of the novel.

9. Jones, C. A. "Galdós's Second Thoughts on *Doña Perfecta*", *Modern Language Review,* LIV (1959), 570-573. An important study of the early editions.

10. Lowe, Jennifer, "Theme, Imagery and Dramatic Irony in *Doña Perfecta*", *Anales Galdosianos,* IV (1969), 49-53. An excellent study of the theme of death and of the imagery of the novel.

11. Nimetz, Michael. *Humor in Galdós. A Study of the 'Novelas contemporáneas'.* New Haven and London, 1968. A mature account of the author's comic vein. *Doña Perfecta* does not figure prominently.

12. Schraibman, Joseph. *Dreams in the Novels of Galdós.* New York 1960. A useful catalogue of the dreams to be found in the novels, with a section on *Doña Perfecta.*

Historical Background .

13. Carr, Raymond. *Spain 1808-1939.* Oxford, 1966. A masterly account of the historical background to the novel.

Galdós's Political Writings

14. *Crónica de la quincena,* ed. W. H. Shoemaker. Princeton, N.J., 1948. With a valuable preliminary study.

15. Hinterhäuser, Hans. *Los 'Episodios nacionales' de Benito Pérez*

Galdós. Madrid, 1963. Apart from its principal purpose, this work studies Galdós's political writings in relation to the historical background.

16. Regalado García, Antonio. *Benito Pérez Galdós y la novela histórica española: 1868-1912.* Madrid, 1966. Includes a further discussion of Galdós's political writings. A necessary corrective to the study is the review article by Raymond Carr published in *Anales galdosianos,* III (1968), 185-189.

17. Glendinning, Nigel. "Psychology and Politics in the First Series of the *Episodios Nacionales*", in *Galdós Studies,* ed. J. E. Varey (London, 1970), 36-61. Considers the relationship of the early writings to the historical background.